PARALLEL
METAVERSES

How the US, China, and the Rest of the World Are Shaping Different Virtual Worlds

GW00645021

NINA XIANG

Copyright © 2022 by Nina Xiang

All rights reserved. No part of this publication may be reproduced, distributed, or transmitted in any form or by any means, including photocopying, recording, or other electronic or mechanical methods, without the prior written permission of the publisher, except in the case of brief quotations embodied in critical reviews and certain other noncommercial uses permitted by copyright law.

For permission requests, please refer to https://www.ninaxiang.com

Sold by: Amazon Digital Services LLC
Language: English

First Edition

Imprint: Independently published

To: 温客行

Contents

Introduction

Writing this book was an unusual experience, and a bit different than the research and processes I followed for my previous books. The subject of this book is the metaverse, whose exact definition is still being debated. Usually, writing a book requires an inordinate amount of time reading through shelves of books, reports, and historical records on a subject. Yet, the pool of existing research materials on the metaverse is still nascent and limited. There are a few books on the metaverse, but they provide very little reference value to assist my comparative studies approach to the topic. There are several dozen research reports in both English and Chinese, most of them were compiled and edited over the past few months. The most helpful research method I therefore used was interviewing industry insiders, and this also was the key research component for my past books. Yet, each person's understanding of the metaverse is different and focused on their own approach. So it's hard to do cross-comparisons.

The biggest chunks of references I used for this book are news reports, which often date a few days or a few months prior to the time of writing. Readers know that the footnote section of a book is normally a walk through the centuries. Not so for this book. A giant exclamation mark illuminated brightly in my head each time I jotted down a footnote that was from a news report a day earlier or sometimes even on the same day! The metaverse space is evolving so rapidly that information needs to be constantly updated. The reincarnated concept of the metaverse in 2022, despite the term being coined initially in 1992, is having its history being written before our eyes.

This, of course, does not mean that there is a lack of information about the metaverse or related ideas. Compared to someone writing a book before the internet age whose key challenge may have been unfriendly librarians, book-writing in the 21st century faces the opposite dilemma: there is too much raw data. It's easy to fall into data rabbit holes. For example, want to learn about computer graphics? There is a seemingly limitless number of articles, reports, websites, news articles, YouTube videos, podcasts, company live-streaming events, Quora and Reddit discussion threads – all at your fingertips. How to make sense of all the raw data becomes the number one task for an author.

That is what I believe is the value of this book. I've fallen down all the data rabbit holes and reemerged, hopefully, with a balanced take on the hottest topic *du jour*. Utilizing my decades-long experience as an award-winning journalist and book author, I've cut through the hype and the self-indulgent fantasies to present a cool-headed analysis of what's being dubbed as "the next chapter of the internet." As an observer, I've consciously kept my distance from the industry to remain independent and mindful of the darker side of things that tech billionaires don't want people to think about.

The metaverse is an evolving concept at a very early stage of its development. The opinions in this book may be controversial, especially because they attempt to make wide-reaching and hopefully useful conclusions. The purpose of this book is not to convince readers of certain convictions, but rather to present the evidence and my own perspective so that readers can make up their own minds. I try to be a critic of the metaverse, not only because there is a very strong basis for caution, but because the utopian voices generated by the industry are so powerful. Even if I may appear to be overly critical, the outcome, I hope, is a metaverse that is healthier, safer, fairer, and greener.

With these caveats outlined, here are the main conclusions of this book:

1. There won't be one metaverse, but rather many metaverses existing in parallel.

Some people believe there should be "one" metaverse where many virtual worlds exist inside that one mega-metaverse. The attraction of such an idea is obvious. The metaverse should be based on the principle of openness and interconnectedness to allow users to "teleport" from one virtual world to another seamlessly. Virtual assets like pets or clothing should be able to move among different virtual worlds effortlessly too. Wouldn't it be nice for billions of people to live in one virtual universe peacefully as a big family?

But this is the most idealized version of how society or the internet operates. Judging by what tech companies are doing at this early stage, it's clear that they want to keep their walled gardens up for as long as they can. Moreover, countries like China would certainly not let their version of the metaverse be open to unfiltered external content. Due to different legal and regulatory requirements in each country, metaverse platforms will likely need to create different versions of their products to meet local requirements, much as how Apple's app stores need to have different versions for each country or market in the real world.

Additionally, a war of tech titans is already in full swing with a dozen or so tech platforms carving up the future "3D internet" into little virtual feudal kingdoms. It's already a headache for content creators to navigate a dozen or so hardware devices like virtual reality headsets. In the end, there will be many metaverses existing in parallel around the world, with some having a more closed and some more open ecosystems. The degree of interconnection will also fall across a wide spectrum. The metaverse, most likely, will mirror the messy and chaotic nature of our physical world.

2. The metaverse will ride on the existing rails of the internet.

It will be akin to adding a third floor to a two-story house, the first floor being the internet and the second floor being the mobile internet. The changes the metaverse will bring are similar to the shift from the internet to the mobile internet: new applications, new business models, and new tech giants will emerge, but existing powers such as Meta, Microsoft, and Tencent will probably safely make the metaverse transition, keeping their dominant positions like they have done so during the mobile internet transition.

In other words, the metaverse will be one factor contributing to the redrawing of the world's tech map, but the major continents and oceans won't shift significantly. Such probability is more likely when one considers the impact of the metaverse will be felt gradually over decades as the technology advances and matures slowly. As regulators around the world curtail the powers of big tech, these new rules present a much more immediate and meaningful risk than the metaverse to the existing tech landscape.

3. Blockchain-based metaverse will only play a marginal or minor role.

Correspondingly, the metaverse will not be decentralized, and NFTs (non-fungible tokens) will not become the main mechanism of value transactions in the metaverse. Some people have been calling for the metaverse to be based on the blockchain technology, to be decentralized, and to rely on NFTs as the basis for value exchanges. It will supposedly give more control and protection to the users and avoid the metaverse from being dominated by big tech.

It all sounds nice, and there will be some space for these types of blockchain-based metaverses to attract users gravitating toward these ideas. But at the meta level [pun intended], these technologies will only play a marginal to minor role. It is because these technologies face many challenges, and it's hard to see them capable of supporting a metaverse ecosystem with billions of users and potentially trillions of market value in the next decade. Not to mention China, one of the two metaverse gravitational centers, will not favor blockchain-based metaverses or allow NFTs to flourish. Judging from the foundations on which big tech have laid down to build their metaverses, they are certainly not placing all their bets on the blockchain.

4. Games will be the starter and the main course of the metaverse banquet.

This means games will likely be the first experience most people will have in the metaverse, and it will be the biggest application in the metaverse. The ideas of a metaverse, often defined as virtual humans interacting in virtual worlds in the most basic form, have been around in games for decades. In fact, the current debate of what constitutes a metaverse is confusing to those in the gaming industry because, for them, the metaverse is what they have been already building for a long time.

Concurrently, the powerful game engines on which it will be critical for creators to build all sorts of metaverses are a derivative product of the gaming industry. Needless to say, games will be one of the biggest markets for the metaverse. Revenue from virtual gaming worlds could grow to over US$400 billion by 2025 from US$180 billion in 2020, accounting for a significant portion of potential metaverse market value.[1]

5. The road toward the metaverse will be a long, rocky journey.

The technology and infrastructure required for the metaverse, from more powerful computing capabilities to faster and more smooth rendering effects, will need to be more significantly advanced. This presents great challenges but also attractive opportunities for companies that can solve technology problems.

More importantly, the metaverse will take decades to be built during a time of potentially chaotic geopolitical upheavals and uncertain regulatory actions against tech companies. In China, for example, tech companies are mostly keeping a low profile in the metaverse chorus as they attempt to absorb the regulatory earthquakes that have shaken the foundation of some companies' business models. How the U.S.-China tech rivalry will continue to evolve is going to impact the degree of connectedness between the two countries' future virtual worlds. Currently, the planned metaverse products by Chinese companies are still based on the Qualcomm/Android framework. Any deterioration of the two countries' relations could hasten China's effort for seeking alternative roadmaps.

As metaverse technologists blur the lines between reality and fantasy, the legal, regulatory, and ethical risks are heightened. As much as big tech companies tout the potential awesomeness of the metaverse, there are concerns, worries, and warnings of which we should be mindful. The last chapter of this book provides an overview of these risks for builders, creators, and users.

This book has five chapters. The first chapter covers the debate about the definition of the metaverse. All relevant ideas are presented to let readers have a broad understanding of all the angles that have been explored. The second chapter is the most important section, where metaverse development in the U.S., China, and the rest of the world is described in detail with a focus on what the big tech companies are accomplishing. The third chapter looks at four components of the metaverse: XR hardware, game engines, virtual humans, and blockchain technology. Each is singled out and highlighted in its own sub-chapters. The fourth chapter explores potential areas where business opportunities exist for founding teams, professionals, companies, and investors. The last chapter lays out a vast array of potential metaverse risks and challenges.

This book is organized in a friendly and indexable manner to better serve readers' different interests and focuses. Some readers may be familiar with a particular market already and may want to learn about development in another region or a particular submarket. They may focus on reading only the portions that match their needs. Each chapter and subchapter are organized to stand alone. As such, some of the same content may be highlighted and reviewed from various angles in different chapters.

Of course, this book is a best effort at providing a comprehensive review of the burgeoning metaverse space based on the limited resources and materials currently available. There may be errors and critical omissions. Because the metaverse is evolving rapidly and new things happen daily, there will be areas of this book that may be outdated at the time of the publication.

But if this book can succeed in helping readers obtain a better understanding of the "big bang" that launched the metaverse and help readers make decisions, whether it's a startup idea or a career move, or a business strategy formulation, it is well worth the effort.

Finally, I want to thank the hundreds of thousands of content creators who wrote articles and blog posts; who made videos and podcasts; and who contributed to building a vibrant, knowledge cyberspace that makes this book possible. That is the power of the internet, which is now making the power of the metaverse possible.

Chapter 1. A Metaverse Reincarnation

What is the metaverse? A most unusual aspect of what is supposed to be the next defining disruptive technology is the lack of a coherent definition. The definitions of the word "metaverse" are much more divergent compared to previous technologies such as "dot com" or "artificial intelligence". It seems a thousand people have a thousand different definitions of how to define the metaverse.

Let's start with people who are going to help build it, as a wide range of such business leaders hasn't been shy in sharing their interpretations. Mark Zuckerburg, CEO of Meta Platforms (formerly Facebook, Inc.), said the metaverse is "the successor to the mobile internet," "the next chapter of the internet," "an embodied internet," and "immersive, all-day experiences."[2]

Microsoft CEO Satya Nadella said the "Metaverse is essentially about creating games," while also acknowledging that it is "the next platform," "the next internet," "the embodied presence"[3] and a "3D world."[4]

Retired Disney CEO Bob Chapek called the metaverse "internet 3.0," and a "more compelling," "more immersive and dimensional" experience.[5]

Jensen Huang, CEO of a dominant chip designer, Nvidia, thinks the metaverse is "a 3D extension of the internet" and predicted that it will be much bigger than the 3D physical world people live in today. Huang said the metaverse could hopefully save "hundreds and hundreds and hundreds of billions of dollars" for companies via virtual simulation.[6]

Co-founder and CEO of a popular game maker, Epic Games, Tim Sweeney, said that the metaverse is a "multi-trillion-dollar" opportunity: "I do believe in this future of the world in which billions of people are wearing AR hardware, AR glasses are their everyday life and I believe that's the entertainment platform of the future."[7] Sweeney also says the metaverse is a broad concept just "like the internet," and therefore "no company can own it."[8]

Matthew Ball, a metaverse thought leader and co-founder of the first New York Stock Exchange Traded Fund (ETF) themed on the metaverse, says it's hard to describe the metaverse, just like "it was hard to envision in 1982 what the Internet of 2020 would be."

But he identified a number of core attributes of the metaverse: persistent; synchronous and live, without any cap to concurrent users; a fully functioning economy; an experience spanning both the digital and physical worlds; interoperable; and populated by experiences created by contributors.[9]

Pony Ma, CEO of Chinese social media giant Tencent, came up with a concept called "Quanzhen (all-encompassing and real) internet" in 2020. He predicted that the Quanzhen internet would be the next big reshuffle and upgrade of the internet sector. As the "unification of online and offline," "the fusion of the physical and the digital," and "the door to both the virtual and the real worlds,"[10] the Quanzhen internet sounds like Ma's vision of the future virtual world before the word metaverse became the de facto designation of such a concept.

An article published on China's Central Commission for Discipline Inspection described the metaverse simply as the "3D internet." It also acknowledged that there is no consensus yet for a definition of the metaverse and "there are one thousand metaverses in the eyes of one thousand people."[11]

Yet, it's easy to see some common keywords among the different definitions given by today's tech leaders. First, the metaverse is recognized as the next chapter, or extension, of the internet. After first transmitting text and images during Web 1.0 (internet), then adding videos and live steaming during Web 2.0 (mobile internet), the next revolution of the internet will provide immersive, real-time experiences that people can feel - ideally with all five senses - instead of simple media that people can only read, watch and hear. And to use a computer file system analogy, it's the difference between only having Read and Write access to also being able to Execute.

Many metaverse platform experiences today are often slow and bug-ridden. They are in a primitive stage that feels like the internet during the 1990s when it often took over 30 seconds to establish a connection. There is enormous potential for improvements and enhancements over the next several decades to reach the ideal version of the metaverse as described by these tech leaders. Therefore, huge opportunities exist for those who can contribute to this process.

Second, the metaverse is a 3D, real-time, synchronous, and immersive internet. It can also be called an experiential internet, or the internet of experience. Most images and videos on today's computer and smartphone screens are still 2D, often asynchronous, and mostly not real-time. The metaverse will mirror the physical world and provide 3D, real-time, and synchronous actions. Moreover, the metaverse experience will simulate beyond vision and hearing to also include the senses of touch, smell, and taste.

In the 1999 science fiction movie, *The Matrix*, a character described how senses can be simulated: "I know this steak doesn't exist. I know that when I put it in my mouth, the Matrix is telling my brain that it is juicy and delicious." This is what Mark Zuckerberg and Satya Nadella mean when they say the metaverse is "embodied internet" or "embodied experience." Contrary to users logging "on" to the internet, future users will be "in" the metaverse and "experiencing" it in immersive ways that blur the line between simulated and physical reality.

Finally, there exist different outlooks for the relationship between the virtual and the physical world. Tencent's Pony Ma imagined "the fusion of the physical and the digital;" Nvidia's Jensen Huang emphasized the benefits of virtual simulation; while Matthew Ball predicts "an experience spanning both the digital and physical worlds."

Will the metaverse be a separate virtual world that exists on its own, or will it be a mirror of the physical world or both? Will the virtual world impact what happens in the real world, or vice versa? This is a complicated topic and there are many debates currently raging. All of those scenarios are possible and much depends on how technology, competition, geopolitical and regulatory changes continue to evolve.

So those are some of the metaverse builders' definitions of the future virtual world. Let's now look at how the metaverse was described in the 1992 science-fiction novel by author Neal Stephenson, *Snow Crash*, where the word metaverse was first coined. Set in a dystopian United States in the 21st century, the novel's main character Hiro Protagonist delivers pizza in reality, but is a warrior prince in the Metaverse.[12] He is a hacker in both worlds, as described in the book:

"Hiro's not actually here at all. He's in a computer-generated universe that his computer is drawing onto his goggles and pumping into his earphones. In the lingo, this imaginary place is known as the Metaverse. Hiro spends a lot of time in the Metaverse…"

"As Hiro approaches the Street, he sees two young couples…He is not seeing real people, of course. This is all a part of the moving illustration drawn by his computer according to specifications coming down the fiber-optic cable. The people are pieces of software called avatars. They are the audiovisual bodies that people use to communicate with each other in the Metaverse. Hiro's avatar is now on the street, too, and if the couples coming off the monorail look over in his direction, they can see him, just as he's seeing them. They could strike up a conversation: Hiro in the U-Stor-It in L.A. and the four teenagers probably on a couch in a suburb of Chicago, each with their own laptop. But they probably won't talk to each other, any more than they would in reality…"

"He turns off his view of the Metaverse entirely, making the goggles totally transparent. Then he switches his system into full gargoyle mode: enhanced visible light with false-color infrared, plus millimeter-wave radar. His view of the world goes into grainy black and white, much brighter than it was before. Here and there, certain objects glow fuzzily in pink or red. This comes from the infrared, and it means that these things are warm or hot; people are pink, engines and fires are red…"

"Hiro turns his attention to Earth. The level of detail is fantastic. The resolution, the clarity, just the look of it, tells Hiro, or anyone else who knows computers, that this piece of software is some heavy shit. It's not just continents and oceans. It looks exactly like the earth would look from a point in geosynchronous orbit directly above L.A., complete with weather systems—vast spinning galaxies of clouds, hovering just above the surface of the globe, casting grey shadows on the oceans—and polar ice caps, fading and fragmenting into the sea...Something catches his attention...he tries to focus on it. The computer, bouncing low-powered lasers off his cornea, senses this change in emphasis, and then Hiro gasps as he seems to plunge down toward the globe, like a space-walking astronaut who has just fallen out of his orbital groove. When he finally gets it under control, he's just a few hundred miles above the earth, looking down at a solid bank of clouds..."[13]

These descriptions about computer-generated virtual worlds, augmented reality goggles, and virtual simulation of the physical world (Google Earth is inspired by "the Earth" idea in the novel) are all important elements of the metaverse as defined by today's tech leaders. There is no coincidence that metaverse became the word of choice to describe the next revolution of the internet.

While the concepts might have been novel in the 1990s, today's readers would immediately recognize that some of these concepts have already become enmeshed in our lives. Particularly for video gamers, they have been playing games in simulated virtual worlds with other players in real-time for decades. Second Life, a popular online virtual world game launched in 2003, hit one million users in a few years and led experts to announce it would be "the future of the internet."[14] Roblox, one of Wall Street's current favorite metaverse concept stocks and gaming platforms, was created in 2004 and has been attracting players for nearly two decades. VR and AR hardware have been around for decades; avatars and virtual persons have been used by social media platforms and apps; AR apps like Google Maps and Pokémon Go have been popular for a long time, and Asia's most famous virtual singers have held massive global concerts since the 2000s.

In some ways, the metaverse is a new word for old ideas. The hype around the metaverse is perhaps peculiar considering there have been several waves of enthusiasm for virtual reality and augmented reality that invariably dissipated over the years. If we really trace it to the origin, the idea of a fantasy world is as old as human history. From the Garden of Eden, Atlantis, Arcadia, Shangri-La, to Alice in Wonderland and the Wonderful Wizard of Oz, people have always dreamed of a world that exists alongside or beyond the physical reality. In a 16th century Chinese novel about mythologies set in the decline of the Shang dynasty (1600-1046BC), a magic landscape scroll was a 3D mirrored world. When opened, the scroll would become blended with its environment. Used to defeat evil creatures, it would lure unsuspecting troublemakers into the scroll and imprison them inside.

In more recent history, the first commercial flight training simulator called the "Link trainer" was created in 1929. It used motors to mimic turbulence and disturbances, as well as the pitch and roll of the rudder and steering, to train U.S. military pilots. That entirely electromechanical simulator was the beginning of sophisticated computer-generated simulators that are now used across industries.

The idea of virtual reality (VR) was first imagined in the 1930s by science fiction writer Stanley G. Weinbaum as a pair of goggles that let the wearer experience virtual worlds through holographic images, smell, taste, and touch. Since then, VR has transitioned from a massive cinematic booth bigger than an ATM, equipped with speakers, 3D display, fans, scent generators, and a vibrating chair in the 1950s, to a large and scary-looking computer-generated graphics display suspended from the ceiling in the 1960s, to today's lighter, smaller and more convenient headsets that users can pull out from a small box and comfortably wear on the sofa for hours. [15]

Augmented reality (AR), which superimposes virtual information on the physical environment (such as overlaying a terrain with geological information), was first developed in 1968 by Harvard computer scientist Ivan Sutherland. Alongside VR, AR technology advanced during the following decades and became more accessible for ordinary consumers.[16] Despite some high-profile blunders including the Google Glass, the Pokémon Go AR game craze in the summer of 2016 caught the imagination of tens of millions of people for the first time. Nowadays, anyone with a smartphone can access AR apps that place animals in their backyard or help visualize how a piece of furniture fits in a living room.

These elements: simulation, AR, VR, as well as avatars, virtual persons, virtual currency, and virtual goods, are important components of the metaverse. They are the building blocks of the metaverse. But the metaverse as dreamed up by technologists today has many new characteristics, and defining exactly what those are, produces the most confusion for everyone who's trying to understand the concept. Some say the metaverse has more similarities to popular multi-player games such as Fortnite and Minecraft. That is why Ryan Gill, a metaverse thought leader and founder of the Open Meta Association, refers to the metaverse as "the internet built by game developers."[17] It is also why some of the leading metaverse companies today are all gaming firms.

Matthew Ball offers a different explanation: "I define the metaverse…(as) a massively scaled and interoperable network of real-time rendered 3D virtual worlds that can be experienced synchronously and persistently by essentially everyone on Earth, and which supports continuity of key components of data, identity, history, payments, virtual objects, and goods." Ball identified some core attributes of the metaverse. After combining his and some other technologists' visions, below is a list of the most common and important shared characteristics of what the future metaverse should be:

1.1. Be persistent, synchronous, and live.

Being persistent means the metaverse is always on, similar to a never-ending live-stream video. If one user leaves the metaverse, it continues with other users inside still experiencing it. It's different from the internet where a user can pause a video and come back later to continue watching it. The metaverse can't be paused. Being synchronous can be explained by the scene described in *Snow Crash*, in which Hiro is walking down the street and sees two young couples exiting the monorail, and they are also seeing Hiro walking down the street. Each of these people is moving in their correct respective locations displaying their respective actions at precisely the same time and frequency. Being live is easier to understand. Similar to live streaming, when you see another avatar dancing, there is a person somewhere in the world who is dictating that avatar's movements in real-time.

1.2. Massively scaled without any cap to concurrent users.

Today, the number of concurrent players in the most popular video games remains small. Video game Fortnite set a 12.3 million concurrent player record in 2020 during an online concert with American rapper Travis Scott. Other popular games such as Roblox and Minecraft often have over one million concurrent players.[18] Moreover, because of computing power limitations, "sharding" is common. It places a cap on the number of virtual players in one virtual setting to usually dozens of players at one time. There is a huge gap between today's concurrent players/player caps to the idealized version of the metaverse where no cap is needed.

1.3. Interoperability.

This means that virtual identities and other virtual goods can seamlessly travel among virtual spaces. Facilitated by compatibility and standardization, interoperability is the version of the metaverse where everything is interconnected with few barriers to free movement. It includes standardization of protocols, locations, identities, currencies, and beyond. Participants can choose to use the same avatar or trade a digital good across multiple metaverse platforms.

1.4. The metaverse will be an all-encompassing, fully functioning economy.

Metaverse, in its various formats, will completely disrupt online shopping, entertainment, gaming, social networking, leisure, work, education, and healthcare. Consumers will bid farewell to the largely static 2D internet that defines these activities in the mobile internet era. Future consumers will demand more immersive, vastly enhanced 3D real-time experiences for such daily tasks. Metaverse will also find applications in enterprise use cases including manufacturing, transportation, and aviation, as well as public services, infrastructure, and energy supply, even helping manage the climate change challenge. People spent US$40.9 billion on buying digital art called non-fungible tokens (NFTs), [19] and gamers spent US$61 billion on in-game purchases such as loot boxes, digital currency packs, and battle passes in 2021.[20] The size of the metaverse economy has been predicted to balloon to around US$800 billion in 2024[21], and US$10 trillion to US$30 trillion in a decade or a decade and a half.[22]

There are other attributes that some people believe are important to the metaverse, such as being decentralized, open, or user-owned. It seems to this author that technologists often get carried away by the potential of new technologies. They seem to believe that new technologies have the capabilities to change everything. But history has shown that people are the ultimate defining factor for how any new technology evolves. Social media companies claimed that connecting people will build stronger communities and even spread democracy. The real consequence is that social media has also divided people even more.

We should remain critical and vigilant when faced with all the rosy predictions of the metaverse like "be experienced...by essentially everyone on Earth;" "without any cap to concurrent users;" "virtual...goods can seamlessly travel between virtual spaces." These are fantasies largely detached from reality. To begin with, 6.5 billion people live on less than US\$30 per day[23] - the definition of poverty in high-income countries – and they are unlikely to afford the metaverse any time soon. Early signs show that complete interoperability among different metaverse ecosystems is impossible.

This author believes a more realistic version of what ultimate shape the metaverse will take is described in the introduction section, that there will be many different versions of the metaverses existing in parallel across the world, that the metaverse will ride on the existing rails of the internet and mobile internet (and therefore be dominated by big tech platforms), and that most of it won't be decentralized.

To summarize, the metaverse in its broadest term refers to the collective existence of everything that shares some of these core attributes and all the encompassing elements that make up the metaverse. Just like the internet relies on software-driven websites, mobile apps, and app stores; platforms like Facebook, Google, and Alibaba; hardware such as personal computers, phones, and broadband cables; and protocols and standards like transmission control protocol and IP addresses, the metaverse is composed of all related hardware, software, platforms, protocols, and standards, as well as content, services, assets, and value exchanges.

In this sense, everything can become a part of the metaverse and doesn't need to possess all the core contributes by themselves. As Matthew Ball explains: "Not every single sub experience will have those [attributes]. There will be virtual worlds inside the Metaverse that don't support continuity of data. There will be experiences within the metaverse that aren't persistent, that are capped to 10 people…But again, they all sit within that broader interoperable framework, much like there are websites that are taken offline, there are websites that have a paywall, there are websites and online communities limited to 10 or 100 people."

In its more narrow definition, metaverse can refer to a specific metaverse platform or application. For example, Meta is building a metaverse where people can use its in-house Oculus Quest VR headset to socialize, work, play and exercise inside the virtual worlds that Meta has built by itself, alongside other content created by independent developers. Meta foresees a future where its metaverse will reach a billion people, and host digital commerce worth hundreds of billions of dollars within the next decade.[24]

Similarly, Roblox, Epic Games, Nvidia, Unity Software, Microsoft, and Disneyland have or are planning to build their own metaverses. Chinese companies including Tencent, Bytedance, and Alibaba have also invested and planned their metaverse strategies, albeit in a more muted manner. Other countries including South Korea have set ambitious objectives for the metaverse.

In the next chapter, we will review what major players in the U.S., China, and beyond are doing to shape their own metaverses.

Chapter 2. The Battle of the Tech Titans

In this chapter, we will review the major companies pursuing the metaverse opportunity in the U.S., China, and the rest of the world. Major companies across the entire metaverse ecosystems from infrastructure technology (5G, cloud computing, semiconductors, etc.) to platform companies (Meta, Microsoft, Google, Tencent, etc.) will be analyzed to provide an overview of the industry landscape in each region.

2.1. The US: Meta, Microsoft, Apple, Google…

The U.S. is the undisputed leader in core advanced technology required to build the metaverse, with the highest number of prominent companies committing the largest amount of capital toward the metaverse. It's the pioneer pushing at the forefront of the metaverse revolution, with the most advanced and complete industrial supply chain to create a powerful metaverse ecosystem. The world is looking at the U.S. as the trend-setter on how the metaverse industry will blossom.

The most prominent player in the U.S. and globally is Meta, which changed it name from Facebook Inc. in November 2021 to shake off a tarnished brand while boldly committing the company's future toward building the metaverse. It plans to spend around US$10 billion over the next year developing the technologies required to make the metaverse a reality. CEO Mark Zuckerberg's vision is "the metaverse will reach a billion people, host hundreds of billions of dollars of digital commerce, and support jobs for millions of creators and developers" within the next decade.[25]

Meta's risky high-profile announcement is what ignited a global metaverse frenzy, but it was a vision that Zuckerberg had in mind and had spoken about repeatedly in the past. In 2014, after Facebook bought virtual reality headset startup Oculus VR for US$3 billion,[26] Zuckerberg already had clear visions of how VR would be much more than a headset:

"After games, we're going to make Oculus a platform for many other experiences. Imagine enjoying a court side seat at a game, studying in a classroom of students and teachers all over the world or consulting with a doctor face-to-face — just by putting on goggles in your home. This is really a new communication platform… Imagine sharing not just moments with your friends online, but entire experiences and adventures."[27]

A metaverse future seemed inevitable to Zuckerberg back then, even if he hadn't attached this word to that vision at that time, but he clearly saw that "immersive 3D content is the obvious next thing after video", images and text.[28]

Meta has invested massive amounts of cash into that vision. Its Reality Labs, the division tasked to build the metaverse, incurred US$21.31 billion losses on US$3.9 billion revenue over a three-year period from 2019 to 2021. This loss is expected to expand in 2022.[29] There are around 10,000 employees working at its Reality Labs, accounting for almost a fifth of the people working at Meta globally[30]. In comparison, the teams in Chinese tech companies are around hundreds of people on average but often much smaller. The company has bought eight VR and AR companies over the years, and more than half of its patent applications since 2019 are related to VR and AR.[31] This scale of capital and human resources investment is unparalleled by any other competitor.

As a result, Meta has one of the most comprehensive, scaled, and advanced technology stacks needed for the metaverse. In hardware, Meta has the most successful consumer VR headset, the US$299 Oculus Quest 2, which sold over 10 million headsets since its release in mid-2019, by one estimate. In comparison, Sony sold about 5.5 million units of its tethered PlayStation VR headset in the fiscal years 2019 to 2021.[32] By another estimate, Oculus had a 75% share in the global VR headset market during the first quarter of 2021.[33] In another sign of Meta's growing clout in the VR headset space, the Oculus was the most downloaded app during Christmas 2021 in the U.S.[34]

Aside from owning the most popular consumer VR headset in the market at this moment, Meta has several other hardware products in the market or in the pipeline. Its smart glasses called Ray-Ban Stories, the result of a cooperation between Meta and Ray-Ban's parent company, was released in 2021 equipped with cameras, voice commands, audio features, and a touchpad. Meta is also working on a high-end standalone headset combining virtual and augmented reality codenamed Project Cambria; a consumer augmented reality (AR) glasses under Project Nazare, and a haptic glove that will let users feel objects. These products are expected to be unveiled to consumers in the coming years.

And the company is researching more far-out futuristic products by developing a wristband that translates motor signals and thoughts from the brain to move virtual objects.

This came after the company ditched earlier plans to develop a mind-reading headset.[35]

In terms of content, Meta has 3.6 billion monthly active users of its various social media applications to mine and convert to its metaverse platforms. To do that, the company needs to build a library of attractive metaverse content. The Horizon platform, which is carved up into different content offerings tailored for different purposes, embodies this effort.

Horizon Home is an entrance space or a welcome lobby, and the first thing users will see when donning their Oculus VR headsets. This is a space where users can socialize. Horizon Worlds is a Second Life-like platform where creators can use the company's VR content creation tools to build user-generated content, such as games, social hangout spaces, escape rooms, and everything else that one can imagine. Horizon Venues lets users watch concerts, sports, and other events within virtual worlds. Horizon Workrooms is for remote work. In Zuckerberg's vision, companies will have virtual offices in Horizon Workrooms with their logos, and employees will work together in this virtual work environment in a more real-life-like experience that is supposedly much better than typical Zoom-based video calls. The Horizon platform, since debuting in December 2021, exceeded 300,000 users in February 2022.[36]

Aside from the Horizon content platforms, the Oculus Store functions like an app store where independent apps are available to Oculus users. The two biggest categories currently are gaming and fitness, and there are over 1,000 apps on the store.[37] A popular VR game Beat Saber, in which users slash flying small cubes, has grossed US$100 million in lifetime revenue on the

Quest platform alone.[38] This will attract more developers to the platform to create more content there. The Oculus Store appears to have the potential to become something akin to Apple's app store, but one specifically made for the metaverse.

One thing worth noting is that Oculus Quest 2 requires a Facebook login, which means users must have a Facebook account to use the Oculus device and content. But the company said in October 2021 that Quest 2 would no longer require a Facebook account starting sometime in 2022 without specifying when the change will be implemented.[39] This is perhaps welcome news to privacy-minded users who either lack Facebook accounts or worry about sharing of data between Oculus and Facebook within the Meta family.

Meta also launched some tools for building metaverse content, including tools helping developers build mixed reality content, real-world 3D reconstruction, AR effects tools, and avatar generators. And the company is betting heavily on educational content, committing US$150 million to train creators to build immersive educational content.[40]

All of these place Meta in its own separate category in terms of its single-minded focus and commitment to bringing a consumer-facing metaverse to life. It will solidify the company's position as a leader if this metaverse strategy is successful but will be devastating otherwise. Nevertheless, the scale of investments and the degree of uncertainty will be a drag on the company in the near future.

Microsoft, on the other hand, is more focused on enterprise applications and mixed reality (MR). In hardware, Microsoft's US$3,500 Hololens MR smart glasses target enterprise applications. This headset has transparent see-through glasses to allow users to maintain their presence in the physical world, unlike VR headsets that block external vision and give users fully immersive virtual experiences. Equipped with hand and eye tracking, with spatial mapping and voice commands, Hololens allows users to conduct various tasks like interacting with 3D digital objects using their hands or reconstructing physical spaces virtually.

These functions are valuable, particularly to the manufacturing, healthcare, and education sectors. Engineers can be trained with Hololens projecting virtual instructions overlaid on physical production lines. Doctors can practice complicated surgeries on virtual patients. Microsoft has reportedly sold tens of thousands of Hololens to companies like auto-makers and coffee machine makers.[41]

One of the biggest customers is the U.S. military, which signed a US$22 billion contract in 2021 for Microsoft to deliver over 120,000 custom-built headsets to the U.S. Army over 10 years.[42] These special-purpose headsets are based on technologies of the Hololens but are elaborately equipped with more features including thermal imagery, GPS, and night vision. Digital information can be overlaid on terrain maps to give soldiers an enhanced understanding of their environment.

These headsets also allow soldiers to change their view vantage point, plan escape routes, locate other team members, see through smoke, and view objects in the dark.[43] There have been delays in this project and rumors that the product has encountered technical challenges,[44] indicating that it will take more time for this technology to be mission-ready.

Microsoft is building up an enterprise-focused platform for the metaverse, launching a mixed-reality collaboration platform in 2021 called Mesh. Mesh works with Hololens 2, most virtual reality headsets, smartphones, tablets, and PCs, allowing users to appear as avatars interacting in virtual spaces. In 2022, Mesh for Teams (Teams is Microsoft's online meeting and conferencing platform) will begin rolling out with features of virtual meetings and social mixers. Microsoft plans to add tools to allow customers to build their own custom spaces (think virtual offices with company logos, exhibition rooms, and custom designs), placing the company in direct completion with Meta in the metaverse remote workspace.

Organized around the Mixed Reality division within its Cloud and AI group, Microsoft's metaverse technology stack also includes Azure Digital Twins, which creates detailed and comprehensive digital models of physical things and places; and Azure IoT, which senses and monitors physical things and connects them to the cloud. Combined with Microsoft's Azure cloud services, these tools provide the needed technologies to converge the physical and digital worlds, which is at the core of Microsoft's enterprise- and MR-focused metaverse strategy.

Microsoft boasts strong capabilities on the consumer market as well, particularly after it announced plans to buy videogame giant Activision Blizzard Inc. for US$75 billion in January 2022. Microsoft already owns a roster of premier game studios behind popular hits like Halo, Fallout, and Minecraft. Its Xbox is among one of the most popular gaming consoles. Combine that with Activision Blizzard's library of popular game titles, Microsoft is one of the largest, most expansive, and diversified multiplayer gaming companies, giving it a solid footing in one of the most important categories of the metaverse.

With its Windows Store, the Xbox game console, and Activision's Battle.net (an online game, social networking, and distribution platform), Microsoft could become a top destination for gamers to discover and find games to play, a position the company is likely to extend to the metaverse era. This places Microsoft in competition with the Epic Game Store and Steam, two major digital game storefronts.

An important feature of Microsoft's metaverse ecosystem is that it is more open and decentralized. Its PC software development remains comparatively more open and more friendly to developers. Its Mesh platform works with a range of external hardware across different systems. In contrast, users must use an Oculus headset to access the Horizon platforms.[45] The company is also developing an identity system that could give users control over their own personal, identifiable information without centralized control of platforms like Facebook or Google logins.[46] This may make Microsoft more attractive to developers and creators, giving it a unique competitive advantage.

Microsoft perhaps forms a stark contrast with iPhone maker, Apple Inc., which is a vertically integrated hardware maker with a somewhat walled-garden ecosystem. In terms of its metaverse strategy, Apple seems to have a different outlook on a philosophical level. Different from the real-time, immersive, always-on virtual worlds envisioned by Meta, Apple is reportedly expecting a different future where mixed reality only serves as short stints of entertainment, gaming, communication, or other specific purposes.[47]

Apple, in fact, tries to avoid using the term metaverse and prefers words like "extended reality" or "mixed reality". But it concurs that going virtual is the future. CEO Tim Cook sees "a lot of potential" in the "critically important" virtual reality space and said the company is investing accordingly. The company notes with pride that it already hosts 14,000 AR kit apps in its App Store providing AR experiences for millions of people.[48]

The most impactful move from Apple, the world's best consumer hardware company, would be on the hardware side. Apple has not released any information, in keeping with its secretive company culture, but there have been rumors of Apple potentially releasing a VR/AR headset as early as the end of 2022. It could be a VR, AR, or mixed reality (MR) headset, which brings together the real world and digital elements. It could come with fancy features such as typing in the air with a virtual keyboard or sharpening part of the field of vision according to where users' eyes are looking (think of a camera that reads your mind placing the focus of the picture where your eyes are looking at while blurring the periphery).[49]

Apple is also rumored to have AR glasses in the pipeline offering optical see-through AR experiences. The glasses will "bring information from your phone to your face," which can display data such as texts, emails, maps, and games over the user's field of vision by synchronizing with their iPhone. Apple's patent records suggest that its AR glasses could offer functions like a better vision in the dark, 3D maps, and holograms of virtual objects.[50] Other reports suggest that Apple AR devices are equipped with micro-organic light-emitting diode (OLED) displays and M1 chip, Apple's self-developed system-on-chip. It will be running Apple's own iOS operating system.[51]

Further out into the future, digital holograms could potentially replace all of the screens people use today. There will be true science fiction style of products that bring seamless convergence of the real and virtual worlds. Apple is reportedly working on this too, albeit at an experimental stage now and could take a long time to materialize.

No other company has the ability to make consumer hardware at the scale of Apple. So when the Apple VR/AR/MR headset or Apple Glass is released to the market, it will be a pivotal moment for the metaverse and potentially make it something authentically mainstream. It will also heighten competition and greatly change the competitive landscape.

Aside from maintaining its dominance on hardware, Apple's App Store may continue to serve as the platform hosting XR (an umbrella term covering VR, AR, and MR) content for Apple users. Apple also offers in-house tools, including Xcode, 3D graphics API Metal, Apple Maps, and AR application development framework ARKit, to developers and creators to build XR content. It's unclear if Apple will go into XR content creation itself. No matter the answer, Apple can rest assured that there won't be a lack of great content from eager developers catering to Apple's massive global user base.

Another core advantage of Apple is its self-developed proprietary chip that will power its XR products. Apple's M1 chip series will afford its future XR devices an unparalleled competitive edge compared to rivals like Meta that rely on commodity chips from third parties. Custom-designed with a system-on-chip architecture, Apple's M1 chips are faster, more efficient, have larger memory bandwidth, and overall provide much better performance. These features matter more, particularly on a head-mount product.

It's worth noting that both Meta and Microsoft are hiring specialists in areas including chip engineering and artificial intelligence chips,[52] indicating that both companies may be following Apple's footsteps to develop in-house semiconductor expertise. But the time-consuming nature of the semiconductor industry means it will take time for them to catch up with Apple.

After reviewing what Meta, Microsoft, and Apple are doing in the metaverse, it's clear that existing tech companies are shaping their strategy according to their technological DNA and based on their existing technological advantages. Meta, as an advertising-based company, aims to maintain its social networking prowess in the era of the metaverse. Its effort to sell Oculus VR headsets at a very low price (some speculate it is well below cost[53]) and to go all-in early on the metaverse is designed to capture users at scale to maintain its position as the de facto social platform. It will in turn ensure it remains a dominant ad placement destination.

Apple, on the other hand, is focusing on maintaining the dominance of its hardware and fitting the metaverse into its vertically-integrated and walled-garden ecosystem. Meanwhile, Microsoft is stacking the metaverse atop its open Windows system, attempting to carve out a niche enterprise AR market, while buttressing it with an impressive gaming assets library in both content, hardware, and distribution.

It is no surprise that Google would follow the same rationale. As a proud tech pioneer, Google has its own preferred word, "ambient computing," to refer to the concept of the metaverse. Its CEO Sundar Pichai agrees that the next chapter of the internet will be more intuitive and immersive:

"It's always been obvious to me that computing over time will adapt to people than people adapting to computers. You won't always interact with computing in a black rectangle in front of you. So, just like you speak to people, you see and interact, computers will become more immersive. They will be there when you need them to be. So, I have always been excited about the future of immersive computing, ambient computing, AR."[54]

Google is one of the earliest tech companies to launch a mass-market AR product. Its AR smart glasses called Google Glass, which allowed users to take pictures, videos and view content via a pair of normal-looking eyeglasses, started selling to a select group of people in 2013. But it had to stop the product rollout in 2015 amid privacy concerns.

In 2017, Google Glass pivoted to focus on enterprise applications. Its Google Glass Enterprise Edition was deployed in factories to help workers read manuals and watch instruction videos via voice commands while working on certain components, for example. Since then, the enterprise product has been expanding its viability to education, healthcare, and other sectors, but there are no estimates on how sales are going. In this market, Google competes with Microsoft's Hololens for the same clientele at a different price range (Google Glass is US$999 and Microsoft's Hololens is US$3,500).

Google's foray into VR, however, seems to have ended with a complete exit. Google Cardboard, a low-cost cardboard viewer in which users can insert their smartphone inside to view VR content, was released in 2014. After scoring over 160 million Cardboard-enabled apps downloads and selling over 15 million viewers over the next few years, Google developed an enhanced VR viewer called Daydream in 2016. But due to poor reception and dwindling interests, Google stopped the Daydream project in 2019 and stopped selling Cardboard viewers in 2021.[55]

Despite these setbacks and a clear rejection of Meta's focus on shut-eye immersive VR experience, Google continued pushing toward "ambient computing". Its 2020 acquisition of smart glasses startup North Inc. suggests that the search engine giant is firmly committed to the internet's next metamorphosis. In 2021, Google unveiled Starline, an experimental video chat booth that allows users to see real-life 3D models of the other person. People sit in something like a photo selfie booth and can see the other person as if they are really right there without wearing any headset, providing another technological roadmap toward immersive experiences without having to strap something on the head. Starline is currently only available in some Google offices, but the company plans to deploy the product first with partners in the healthcare and media sectors.[56]

At the same time, Google is building AR content and services that work both on mobile and smart glasses. Google Maps Live View overlays directions, street signs, and landmarks over the real world to help users navigate. Google Lens can scan and identify plants, images, buildings, and text, and it can also translate from one language to another. These apps, already running on hundreds of millions of phones, could continue to make Google the primary information filter and organizer during the metaverse age.

That is consistent with Google's timeless mission of focusing on "search." As CEO Pichai said, "Being able to adapt to all that (changes in man-machine interaction) and evolve search will continue to be the biggest opportunity" for Google.[57] The search engine giant is likely to continue serving as the place for users to discover and organize information in the future virtual world.

There are many more American companies deploying XR technology and developing metaverse strategies. Amazon's AR shopping tool allows users to use phones or tablets to see how furniture would fit in their homes. IKEA offers a similar tool. Walmart toyed with the idea of VR shopping in 2017, and Disney has appointed a new executive in charge of the company's metaverse effort.

Predictably, companies will be announcing new metaverse initiatives this year with the kind of excitement back in the 2000s when Second Life attracted fashion brands like Adidas and Calvin Klein to its virtual worlds. This new wave of enthusiasm uncannily echoes the plot of *Snow Crash*. The novel described the phenomenon that an expression, the "metaverse" for example, is like a virus that spreads exponentially. In fact, metavirus, the computing virus in the book, is described as an atomic bomb of informational warfare that caused any system to infect itself with new viruses. Metaverse is the newest "language virus" in 2022 that will infect every boardroom, newsroom, and company headquarters around the world.

There will be a lot of empty talk and vaporware, but there will also be a real and exciting technological innovation that's going to revolutionize industries. A few more companies deserve special mention. American chip designer Nvidia has built an impressive platform combining its industry-leading hardware (Nvidia GPU and DPU chips)[58] and software acumen to create what it calls the Omniverse. It is a cloud-based 3D collaboration platform incorporating numerous third-party tools that can become a one-stop shop for companies, creators, and developers to create high-quality virtual worlds.

Virtual world creation tools will be very important. Building a virtual universe as diverse – or even more diverse - than the real world, requires tools to enable every person to participate in the task of re-creating the "Book of Genesis" digitally. Different from an omnipotent God who created the world in seven days, the metaverse must be built by a large number of people collaboratively. Therefore, the creation tools must be accessible, efficient, and easy to use.

Nvidia's Omniverse is such a one-stop destination for developers and creators to access not only Nvidia's own tools, but also third-party tools. The objective is to incorporate as many third-party tools onto Omniverse as possible and to pool different ecosystems together. Currently, a developer can create one avatar in Epic Games' Unreal Engine (a game creation tool), but may not be able to use that avatar in a different game engine. Omniverse is trying to solve that problem by attracting all the major creation tools to join its platform.

In addition, Omniverse has many useful enterprise applications due to its excellent physics engines. In one example,

BWM Group used Omniverse to create digital twins of its factories. A digital factory is an exact digital copy of the physical factory, and can therefore simulate new plant layouts and factory throughput, among other things. Experimenting and perfecting methods in the digital factory will lead to the implementation of the best solution in the physical factory. Hypothetically, if Elon Musk had a digital twin of his Tesla factory back in 2018, he could have avoided a costly and nightmarish "production hell" that saw the factory only deliver less than half of its projected production of Model 3.

In another instance, Omniverse showcases a virtual robot bursting into a 3D display of all its parts floating midair. Users can zoom in on any particular component to see how it connects with other parts and how it looks when it's in motion. This can be extremely useful in manufacturing. Omniverse also demonstrates its incredible effect of simulating particles and fluids, as well as other materials, to photo-realistic quality. Think about the 1999 science fiction movie hit, The Matrix's famous bullet-dodging scene. Back then, it required 120 cameras to shoot the scene and dozens of artists working on the post-production to create that iconic shot. With Omniverse, or other similar software from companies like Epic Games' Unreal Engine and Unity, it can be created digitally with much less time and resources.

Similar to Nvidia's Omniverse, Unity and Unreal Engine (the world's biggest and second-biggest game engines, respectively)[59] operate in an area where Chinese companies lag behind both in technology and scale. American game engines (despite its game-related name, the technology has many more applications including in filmmaking, manufacturing, and healthcare) have a duopoly in the global game engine market.

Unity and Unreal Engine are capable of creating more realistic scenes with detailed lighting, shadows, geometry construction, and more detailed and realistic actions on a level that Chinese companies cannot yet reach. Chinese game developers say that it is difficult for Chinese companies to simulate simple actions, like jumping, very well. Chinese company Tencent owns 40% of Epic Games, which owns Unreal Engine. But U.S. regulators have been looking into potentially having Tencent exit its investments in American game companies due to national security concerns.[60]

Gaming is very important for the metaverse, not only as the earliest and the largest application but also as a key source of technology to build the metaverse. Some American companies including Roblox, Minecraft, and Fortnite are recognized as having already built initial versions of the metaverses successfully. There are many shared characteristics between the massively multiplayer online role-playing game (MMORPG) and the metaverse. Both are set in virtual worlds involving multiple players interacting with each other. Both involve virtual identities, avatars, buying and selling of virtual goods, and user-generated content.

Roblox ignited an investor frenzy when it completed a direct listing on the New York Stock Exchange in March 2021, boosting a market capitalization of nearly US$40 billion.[61] Dubbed as the first IPO of a metaverse company, Roblox lets users create their own virtual homes, virtual games, and virtual experiences on the company's gaming platform, which is very similar to Second Life. But because the majority of Roblox's users are under the age of 16, the most popular Roblox games involve kid-friendly role-playing such as adopting digital pets or building houses. It has grown popular, particularly during the Covid-19 pandemic, and has been recognized as exemplifying the potential of the metaverse.

While most of the MMORPGs are played on computers and mobile devices, Roblox, Minecraft, and Fortnite are all available on VR. Games will be a core application of the metaverse and how most people initially will get into the future virtual worlds. The U.S. has a very robust ecosystem in games. The same cannot be said of China, where no new games have been approved for release since July 2021, and Tencent's attempt to bring Roblox and Epic Games' Fortnite to China has failed.

Next, we will review how China's big tech companies are formulating their metaverse strategies.

2.2. China: ByteDance, Tencent, Baidu, Alibaba…

The Chinese economy is driven by government policy. To understand China's metaverse ecosystem, the starting point of analysis must be a look at how Beijing understands the technology and how government policy is likely to be formulated. Until now, China has not officially stated its opinion on the metaverse or included the word in any central government-issued official government documents. Such inclusion usually signals official national-level validation and support.

Perhaps the metaverse hasn't been a priority for China's policymakers. The country's economy is at a delicate spot after a painful slowdown due to the Covid pandemic and deleveraging amid geopolitical tensions. The country's tech companies are increasingly viewed by international investors as "uninvestable" or "quasi-public service" platforms after continuous regulatory crackdowns and public censures. Over US$1 trillion in market value has been wiped out of China's publicly listed tech companies. Tense relations between the U.S. and China, complicated further by a Russia/Ukraine conflict, risk further deterioration. It may push China's tech ecosystem to decouple more broadly from the rest of the world.

In the backdrop of this volatile setting, there are signs that China will take a pragmatic and utilitarian approach toward the metaverse, consistent with how it treats tech innovations historically. Beijing will embrace the metaverse as long as it serves the country's goals of economic development and social stability, while incorporating strict measures to curtail any potential harm such as fraud and "excessive capital expansion" (code word for market manipulation).

Specifically, Beijing will encourage any applications of the metaverse that support the growth of the "physical economy", and look less favorably on applications that are purely virtual and deemed not adding value. It will emphasize the utilitarian values of the metaverse (helping factories be more productive, for example), while weakening the metaverse's function as a financial product. That is behind Baidu's considerations for not offering any virtual land for sale when it launched its metaverse platform, Xirang.

Chinese state media have published articles showcasing this nuanced approach. A China Daily opinion piece stated that the potential opportunities and possible changes of the metaverse "are worth looking forward to," but the public should be "wary of any irrational exaggeration in the name of technology."[62] Another China Daily piece quoted experts stating that the metaverse provided the possibility that the internet technology can achieve a "paradigm change" after many years of undergoing merely "quantitative changes."[63]

Both pieces are cautious to give any definite official stance on the metaverse and believe that it will take time to truly understand it and its impact. Both warn of the potential risks, as the latter piece wrote that "it is necessary to be alert to issues such as capital manipulation, ethical risks, and the need to strengthen legislative supervision."

These warnings are perhaps redundant, considering China is still in the midst of a thorough crackdown of its once loosely-reined tech sector. After Beijing halted Ant Group's proposed IPO in late 2020, major Chinese tech companies have been fined and punished for anti-competitive and other non-compliant behavior. The passing of two major laws placing strict oversight on how companies handle data security and personal privacy added great uncertainties to tech companies' data-heavy operations, and a new law that went into effect on March 1, 2022, focuses specifically on the way companies use algorithms to display content. A dramatic saga involving Didi's U.S. IPO and its subsequent wrangling with regulators risks the collapse of the Chinese ride-hailing giant.

It is therefore understandable that both state-owned media and Chinese tech titans are rather low-key on the metaverse. But the metaverse frenzy in China is no less feverish, even if companies refrain from making loud announcements of the deals and investments they make behind the curtains. In particular, one group of players isn't shying away from making their ambitions known. Local governments see the metaverse as an opportunity to catapult themselves to becoming China's next Zhongguancun, otherwise known as China's Silicon Valley in Beijing, and a fierce competition is already underway to attract the best talent and companies.

Shanghai was the first Chinese city to include the metaverse in its 14th Five Year Guidelines for its electronics information industry in December 2021. The city of Hefei and Wuhan included the metaverse in their government work report in January 2022 as an industry to cultivate and promote. The city of Wuxi issued a development plan to create China's metaverse ecosystem demonstration zone. Beijing city is pushing to set up an innovation alliance to promote the development of the metaverse, while Shenzhen and Chengdu also have similar plans. The city of Hangzhou has set up a metaverse committee to study policies relating to it. [64]

Judging from the language of these local government policies, China is likely to make metaverse part of its push for the digital economy and the "New Infrastructure" initiative.[65] It will likely be treated similarly to technologies such as artificial intelligence and Internet-of-Things. Technology parks, incubators, and government incentive policies tagging the metaverse concept will likely emerge across the country in a nationwide industrial typhoon.

At the same time, startups labeled as metaverse companies are mushrooming everywhere, and there are increasing investments flowing into the sector as venture capitalists rush to bet on the next "disruptive technology." During the first half of 2021, there were hardly any metaverse startups raising capital. But until the time of writing, there have been 25 venture investments in metaverse startups in China involving hundreds of millions of U.S. dollars.[66]

Anecdotally, there have been an explosive number of private Wechat groups, metaverse study groups, metaverse articles, and metaverse conferences that this author has seen or participated in personally. Even though this frenzy is happening everywhere, it seems to have a more pronounced fear-of-missing-out (FOMO) atmosphere in China due to the country's intensely competitive environment. There are two to three times more metaverse research reports published in Chinese than those in English that this author has read.

Even with a much smaller tech sector, China still boasts a massive domestic market and impressive technological capabilities that put the country as the second most important country for the metaverse. Morgan Stanley predicted that the metaverse market in China alone would become an US$8 trillion market in the future.[67] Similar to the U.S., the existing tech giants will have an outsized impact on how China's metaverse shapes up. They include Tencent, Bytedance, Baidu, Alibaba, and others, which we will review one by one.

Tencent, China's social media and gaming titan, is keeping a low profile on the surface. Its founder and CEO Pony Ma has been discussing the coming age of Quanzhen (all-encompassing and real) Internet since 2020. On the company's quarterly earnings call in November 2021, Ma said that "The metaverse is an exciting topic, and I believe Tencent has a lot of technologies and capabilities to explore and develop the metaverse…in gaming, social media, and artificial intelligence-related fields, we all have rich experience."[68]

Tencent is actively integrating its virtual world building blocks into its existing structures to ensure that it emerges from the next "big tech reshuffle" as the winner again. Tencent boasts an impressive asset pool. Its WeChat app has 1.26 billion monthly active users and is the default communications tool for the majority of the Chinese population. Its WeChat pay has a 38.8% share in China's third-party payment market.[69] Around one-third of Tencent's revenues are from games, and it has a near-monopoly of the Chinese domestic gaming market, with its gaming revenue bigger than the next 20 companies combined.[70] It also owns leading international gaming companies including Epic Games, Riot Games, and Supercell.

Tencent's most prominent move in the metaverse is its partnership with Roblox, the company labeled as metaverse's first IPO. In 2019, Tencent formed a joint venture with Roblox to bring a localized version of the game to the Chinese market. Owning 49% of the joint venture and serving as the sole distributor of Roblox in China, Tencent was hoping to repeat Roblox's success in the world's biggest gaming market: China. In July 2021, the joint venture released the Chinese version of

Roblox on iOS and Android. It jumped to the app store's number one spot for free games on the day and has reached 1.5 million downloads in the next five months.[71]

But five months later, the game abruptly closed its servers and went offline. The official announcement stated that the company hoped to upgrade the game and launch it soon.[72] The sudden manner of the shutdown and the fact the company took the unusual action of deleting player data (meaning players would lose all their personal items, creations, and all other data – very frustrating for any game player) makes the gaming circle speculate that the action may be the result of regulatory pressure.

China has implemented strict measures to protect its youth from gaming addiction and to ensure content compliance. China's National Press and Publication Administration has stopped issuing approval for new games since July 2021. In August 2021, Beijing issued rules to limit minors to only three hours of gaming time a week. China is also undergoing a renewed official campaign to promote "positive content" to "maintain online political security and ideological security", creating a "clean cyberspace"; while prohibiting "unhealthy" and "addictive" content.[73]

Aside from online content, television, and films, games are an important form of content and are subject to these tightened rules. Roblox's model of user-generated-content (UGC), in which independent developers create and publish games on Roblox, might be problematic for Chinese regulators. Roblox is also a game targeting minors, with over half of its current users globally under the age of 16. The gaming time limit placed on Chinese minors would significantly impact Roblox's reach unless the game is meaningfully localized to target a wider audience. Tencent will try its best to bring Roblox to China, but it is highly uncertain if it can succeed.

Another blow to Tencent in the gaming arena is that its effort to bring the popular Battle Royale game Fortnite to China has failed too. In October 2021, the game's Chinese version announced that it would shutter its servers after three years of operating in testing mode on Tencent's WeGame platform. It didn't state the reason, but it appears that the game has failed to obtain official approval despite years of effort.[74]

Tencent owns 40% of Epic Games, the publisher of Fortnite, and the owner of the world's second-largest gaming engine called Unreal Engine. Acting as Fortnite's sole distributor in China, Tencent's latest setback compounds its troubles. The company's stock price has more than halved during the past year due partially to not having new games approved for seven months and counting. Moreover, U.S. regulators have been looking into potentially having Tencent exit its investments in American game companies due to national security concerns.[75]

Despite these setbacks, Tencent is steadily making forays into the metaverse. TiMi Studio Group, an elite games development unit of Tencent Games, began recruiting specialists for a project called ZPlan in 2021. Reported to boast a team of nearly 1,000 people, ZPlan may aim to create games integrating social networking and gaming in virtual worlds. It has generated speculation that this would be Tencent's attempt to create a metaverse blockbuster product. TiMi Studio's lead engine programmer has stated that the studio is building a virtual community similar to the "Oasis" fantasy virtual worlds in science fiction film *Ready Player One* in the long term.[76]

Besides games, in January 2022, Tencent updated its QQ messenger app, which has 574 million monthly active users but is seeing declining user numbers, with Epic Games' Unreal Engine embedded in the app. The move is interpreted to be a metaverse play to include a new feature called Super QQ Show allowing users to socialize in virtual 3D worlds. The Unreal Engine will be critical for rendering the avatars and virtual worlds more realistically for the new feature.

Super QQ Show is similar to what Meta is trying to build with its Horizon suite of VR experiences, with user-generated avatars, games, and social networking. The difference is that Super QQ Show is currently displayed on smartphones and does not require a headset, although it certainly could move toward VR next.

If Super QQ Show is to be Tencent's channel of building up a social networking metaverse platform, the company will no doubt want to extend to hardware. Tencent reportedly lost a bidding war in 2021 to acquire China's leading VR headset maker, Pico, to rival ByteDance, the operator of short video app TikTok. After that, Tencent is rumored to be in deal talks with a number of VR headset makers, including Taiwanese electronics firm HTC, Chinese video platform iQiyi (both have VR headset units), and an independent headset maker, Dapeng VR.[77] A deal to acquire or collaborate with one major VR headset company could be in the works for Tencent.

At the same time, despite having said that it would not get into the hardware business, Tencent reportedly bought a niche game phone maker called Black Shark Corporation in January 2022.[78] Black Shark's phones are customized for playing mobile games. But its hardware expertise could be useful if Tencent decides to launch its own hardware for the metaverse, whether it's VR, AR, or a combination of the two. Black Shark is reportedly tasked with developing a VR headset for Tencent after the acquisition.[79] All these seem to point to Tencent extending to XR hardware in some manner, most likely via an independent business unit or via external partnerships.

Tencent has also registered over 20 metaverse-related trademarks, including those relating to its hit games such as "Game for Peace" and "Honor of Kings." The company is reportedly developing some kind of VR versions of these popular games too.[80]

In addition, Tencent has its own game engine called Quicksilver but it is only open for internal use. China's game engine market is very different from the U.S. This topic will be explored in later sections. Tencent, as the social media and gaming giant, has a metaverse strategy focused on leveraging these two core advantages while making up its weakness of hardware. A more ambitious outlook for Tencent's product matrix could be a complete suite of hardware, software, content, and platforms.

ByteDance is assembling a similar blueprint to Tencent and Meta. The company acquired a VR headset maker called Pico in August 2021. Pico was the third-largest virtual reality headset maker globally in the first quarter of 2021.[81] The acquisition, rumored to be around RMB5 billion (US$790 million) to RMB9 billion (US$1.42 billion) gave ByteDance an instant lead in taking a sizeable market share in the entrance device for the metaverse compared to other Chinese tech giants.

Pico has an interesting connection to Meta's Oculus. Founded in 2015, Pico is incubated inside the Chinese company Geortek Inc, the manufacturer of Oculus. Geortek is a major Original Equipment Manufacturer (OEM) to companies like Apple, Huawei, and Xiaomi. Pico's founder Zhou Hongwei was previously the vice president of Geortek.[82] Pico's sales are much smaller at around half a million cumulative shipments. In comparison, Oculus has sold as much as 10 million units by one estimate.[83] Given China's market scale and Chinese companies' execution prowess, however, Pico's sales volume could grow exponentially to close the gap with Oculus in the next several years.

With 1.9 billion monthly active users across many video and news apps, ByteDance certainly wants to keep gluing billions of eyeballs to its products. In January 2022, it launched an internal testing version of metaverse social networking app in China called Party Island. Just like Meta's Horizon Worlds and Tencent's Super QQ Show, it allows users to generate their own avatars and socialize in its virtual worlds. A few months earlier, ByteDance launched a similar app called Pixsoul in Southeast Asia.[84]

The linkage between Pico device and ByteDance's virtual world content is not yet integrated under one umbrella, like Meta's Oculus ecosystem. ByteDance's metaverse content apps are also in a more initial development stage compared to Meta's Horizon Worlds. There are fewer apps and games available and they are still in internal testing modes. It is only natural considering that Meta has hundreds of times more people working on its metaverse products and are investing capital that is exponentially more than its Chinese peers.

ByteDance is going to accelerate integrating different assets to establish a streamlined metaverse product matrix, however. Aside from the hardware and content assets, ByteDance invested in a couple of digital human and virtual idol startups over the past two years. It also invested in a cloud digital twin company called Zhongqu Tech at the end of 2021. The company focuses on AI machine vision and 3D technology to provide users with immersive space roaming experiences. [85] As the company completes its technology stack buildup, product rollout will likely follow quickly.

Gaming, as the starter and the main course of the metaverse banquet, is an arena that ByteDance has great ambitions in but lacks muscles currently. From 2017 to 2021, ByteDance has acquired 11 mobile gaming companies. It launched its own gaming brand Nuverse in 2021 to integrate all of its gaming assets under one umbrella. The investments have generated some popular games that have grossed billions of Yuan, but are still a long way from building a competitive foothold.[86]

One estimate puts ByteDance's gaming gross billing at around RMB4 billion to RMB5 billion in 2020.[87] That compares to the gaming revenues for Tencent, Netease, and IGG Inc. (the first, second, and tenth biggest gaming companies in China in 2020) of RMB482 billion, RMB73.7 billion, and RMB4.8 billion, respectively.[88]

This is not an accurate comparison, because gross billing and revenue are two different metrics and the ByteDance estimate may not be accurate. But it makes it clear that it will take time for ByteDance to catch up with its Chinese rivals. That's something the company is trying to correct in a hurry, particularly when it comes to gaming in the metaverse.

In April 2021, ByteDance invested in Chinese mobile game developer My Code View, which operates a user-generated-content (UGC) gaming platform letting young users use its game creation tool to develop and publish the games on its platform. For this reason, the company is often referred to as China's answer to Roblox. One month earlier, ByteDance acquired Shanghai-based gaming studio Moonton Technology at a valuation of US$4 billion, once again outbidding Tencent in the deal.[89] Moonton is behind the multiplayer online battle arena (MOBA) game Mobile Legends popular in Southeast Asia. ByteDance's recent deal activities of repeatedly outbidding rivals show that the company is committed to winning a big chunk of the metaverse gaming pie at all costs.

With uncertainties high in the Chinese gaming market regarding obtaining approval for new games, ByteDance has a more pronounced focus on exploring the overseas market. Compared to Tencent's monopoly in China, the overseas gaming market is much less entrenched, giving ByteDance a better chance of success. The next few years will see how successful ByteDance will be in realizing its ambitions in gaming.

ByteDance is also the most internationalized Chinese tech giant, and its overall strategy will have a more global angle. With one billion monthly active users in over 150 countries as of January 2022, the short video app TikTok provides a perfect entry point to the metaverse for ByteDance. In August 2021,

TikTok launched a private beta besting of a creative toolset called TikTok Effect Studio that allows developers to build AR effects for short video apps.[90] The company will predictably launch more XR features on TikTok and many of its overseas products in the future to transition from a video watching app to one providing more immersive experiences. Whether ByteDance can safely complete the metamorphosis will be key for its continued success.

Moving onto Baidu, China's dominant search engine, the picture becomes a bit confusing. As an increasingly marginalized Chinese tech titan, testified by its market capitalization now at only a fraction of its peers, Baidu has suffered from past strategic mistakes. Having spoiled the mobile internet opportunity, Baidu placed its bet on artificial intelligence starting from the mid-2010s. Whether the AI bet will enable a Baidu turnaround is still uncertain, because AI faces a number of challenges including the lack of a proven sustainable business model, Baidu didn't hesitate in jumping onto the metaverse bandwagon.

Baidu is the highest-profile Chinese tech company making forays into the metaverse. In December 2021, Baidu made what it called "China's first metaverse product" available to users. Called XiRang (The Land of Hope), the app is an attempt to create a Horizon Worlds-like metaverse with Chinese characteristics. Featuring both futuristic skyscrapers and historical cultural sites like the Shaolin Temple, users can explore the virtual worlds via their phones, computers and VR headsets. To help generate interests in the app, Baidu held its annual Baidu AI developer conference inside XiRang, claiming its conference center allows 100,000 users to interact with each other at the same time.

The event succeeded in attracting great interests in Baidu and made it the first Chinese company to unveil a relatively "mature" and emphatically labeled metaverse product to the public. Although it seems the company achieved this goal in a rush and at the cost of the product not being fully ready. Participants of the conference complained of glitches, disconnections, dizziness, poor audio quality, and other bugs. The rendering of the virtual space was also rough and not so detail-oriented. The app accumulated nearly 1,500 ratings on the iOS App Store and averaged only 2.2 stars out of 5 stars as of February 2022.[91]

The XiRang project was in fact launched inside Baidu in December 2020, and incorporates many of Baidu's existing technology capabilities including cloud computing, AI, and its personal assistant Xiaodu. The company did a lot of work to achieve an astonishing number of 100,000 concurrent users being able to see and interact with each other at the same time in its conference center. The company said that its Baidu Smart Cloud provided XiRang with PFLOPS-level large heterogeneous computer power, hundreds of GB of bandwidth, and infinitely scalable computing storage to ensure super-large-scale data transmission projects.[92]

This number is jaw-dropping when one considers that Meta's Horizon allows up to 20 people at a time in a virtual space and Rec Room, a popular free VR game, allows up to 40 people in a room.[93] The small number of users allowed per virtual space in today's VR games is because of the massive amount of computing required for rendering virtual spaces and avatars. Normally, after reaching the maximum number of users in one virtual space, companies place users onto different servers to accommodate more users in a practice called sharding.

But the Baidu number shouldn't be taken at face value. This author's understanding from talking to insiders is that the level of user interaction for XiRang is very limited. It is certainly not possible for it to host 100,000 virtual persons in one virtual space with the types of interactions and rendering normally seen on platforms like Horizon Worlds and Rec Room. In fact, even though the conference hall was full with nearly 100,000 avatars filling all the seats, many appear to be just static avatars.

Overall, the XiRang app presents perhaps Baidu's attitude of wanting to reap the maximum potential benefits of the metaverse, yet still being very cautious of making too big a strategic commitment prematurely. Even though the metaverse frenzy has generated a wave of speculative virtual land transactions in China, Baidu refrained from offering virtual land sales inside XiRang. This is of course the result of heeding warning signs from the government after state-run newspapers published articles condemning virtual land speculation.

But still, XiRang app's purpose and positioning are a bit perplexing. Baidu seems to want XiRang to be everything to everybody. The company said that the app's target applications include virtual education, virtual exhibitions, and virtual conferences. In other words, it is geared toward business applications. But it also has characteristics of social networking targeting individual users, in addition to being an all-in-one platform hoping to attract creators and developers to create their own virtual space. It is essentially one virtual world that is expected to function with many different roles, akin to putting Horizon's various offerings into one app. Whether this one-stop strategy can work will need time to tell, but this author is not optimistic.

Aside from XiRang, Baidu has some legacy technologies from its past investments in AR and VR. Its VR assets include VR content creation tools, the VR content display software, and a Baidu VR headset, which is not sold in the market separately. The XiRang app is currently listed under Baidu VR division. This division offers VR services in education, e-commerce, VR ads, VR conferences, and VR training.

The most notable application is Baidu VR "Red Education," which is designed to help companies and organizations meet mandatory study requirements of the history of the Communist Party of China (CPC) in a government drive to strengthen Party solidarity. Some use cases listed on Baidu's website include company employees experiencing the Red Army's Long March in VR donning Baidu's VR headset, and a reconstructed VR exhibition hall of an actual exhibition in Beijing commemorating the CPC's centenary.[94]

Baidu AR is currently part of Baidu Brain, the company's open AI platforms. Based on its AI technologies, Baidu boasts that it has full-suite AR capabilities from space (SLAM positioning, mapping, AR display), content creations (3D rendering engine, avatar generation), to interaction (facial, gesture tracking). These technologies allow the company to deliver AR applications such as VR directions, mapping generation, virtual assistants, and industrial AR.

The company lists dozens of use cases across a wide range of sectors from helping visitors to view exhibitions better at museums to helping workers conduct pipeline inspections more accurately. Baidu Map, with nearly 400 million users, has been offering AR directions for years. The app overlays virtual directions in the physical world viewable from smartphones, similar to functions available on Google Maps.

Baidu has accumulated a comprehensive technology stack for delivering the metaverse, thanks to its many years of dedicated work in artificial intelligence. Yet, it does many things and seems to lack a focused strategy. It currently is without any potential blockbuster application. Unlike its American peer Google, which continues to focus on "filtering and organizing" information, metaverse or not, Baidu seems to want to move into the metaverse product space more forcefully.

Baidu's metaverse strategy seems to be "crossing the river by feeling the stone," a commonly used phase in China to mean perfecting the methods via trial-and-error. Maybe a Baidu executive was honest when he said that the road to the metaverse is long and it will take time to find out how to make the best use of it.[95] For now, XiRang's virtual world is waiting for users, companies, developers, and creators to join and bring it to life. Whether they will come will be a big question mark.

Alibaba, China's e-commerce giant, has a more focused metaverse strategy. Faced with a fierce regulatory crackdown, including the cancellation of its Ant Group IPO, record anti-monopoly fine, an ongoing restructuring, and implications in corruption cases, the company remains cautious and low-key. But behind the scenes, the e-commerce company is working actively to transition to a meta-commerce company, with a focus on the core e-commerce and cloud businesses.

E-commerce is an important application for XR. As early as in 2016, Alibaba's e-commerce platform Taobao launched Buy+, a VR shopping experience. Utilizing computer graphics and sensors, Buy+ allowed users to interact with virtual goods and can automatically generate 3D shopping environments. This feature was upgraded in 2021 to allow this immersive shopping experience accessible from both VR headsets and the phone. In its annual conference at the end of 2021, Alibaba unveiled holographic retail stores where users can walk around a store, click to view product details, and place an order.

Even though e-commerce is the central focus for Alibaba, the company is also exploring other applications. One notable step was establishing an XR Lab under Alibaba's Damo Academy, the company's research unit for basic scientific research and core technology development, in October 2021.

Damo Academy's research is designed to tightly collaborate with Alibaba's businesses. The XR Lab's research areas include all the core capabilities for the metaverse: mapping models, 3D mapping, virtual object visualization, person construction, and virtual information superposition in the physical world. These technologies can be applied in a variety of use cases beyond e-commerce, such as home furnishing (similar to IKEA's use case), industrial manufacturing, robotic training, arts and culture (using AR to view art shows and museums). These use cases were demonstrated by Alibaba at its annual conference in October 2021.[96] But it appears these applications are in an early experimental stage.

Another important step the company took was Alibaba Cloud launching a new platform called Yuanjing to support "cloud gaming" in September 2021.[97] Gaming is the starter and the main course of the metaverse banquet. Revenue from virtual gaming worlds could grow to over US$400 billion by 2025 from US$180 billion in 2020, accounting for a significant portion of potential metaverse market value.[98]

While games in China face great uncertainty relating to obtaining official approvals for new game releases, the exponential demand for computing power with the arrival of the metaverse is a certainty. Not involved in game development itself, Alibaba wants to be the computing capability provider to the anticipated gaming transition to the metaverse. Yuanjing wants to be the infrastructure for cloud games, which it believes will be the prerequisite of super-large-scale open virtual worlds, ultra-high-definition rendering, realistic and rich interactions, as well as allowing as many as 10,000 people to be in the same virtual space.[99]

Aside from claiming to have achieved latency as low as 5 milliseconds via Alibaba Cloud's vast global network, Yuanjing is also constructing collaborative rendering capabilities in the cloud and building up its developer platforms. The ultimate objective of Yuanjing is to provide an all-in-one game platform where games can be developed, distributed, and maintained. This is a relatively safe bet as Alibaba aims to become the "electricity" provider for the metaverse. It also plays into its strength, as Alibaba Cloud is the dominant market leader with a 38.3% market share in mainland China's cloud market.[100]

Alibaba has and is investing in metaverse-related companies. Back in 2016, Alibaba invested in American AR startup Magic Leap. It's also this author's understanding that Alibaba has invested in a Chinese AR glasses maker. In addition, Alibaba established a new company in August 2021 with its business scope covering VR equipment, indicating that the e-commerce giant may go into XR hardware either directly or via a close partnership with an external party.

Alibaba should be able to replicate its success in smart speakers, and intelligent hardware with massive addressable consumer markets (Alibaba is the leader with 35% of the Chinese smart speaker market[101]), with XR headsets if it decides to pursue that channel. Alibaba could become an important player in XR hardware, and the entrance points to the metaverse. It will likely play an important role in providing computing infrastructure for the metaverse, and certainly be the most critical company utilizing metaverse applications in e-commerce.

Almost all major Chinese tech companies have made some movements into the metaverse. Netease, China's second-largest game company and one of China's oldest internet companies, unveiled its own metaverse platform called Yaotai at the end of 2021. Designed to first host events for companies, Netease plans to expand its applications to social networking and other special occasions such as music concerts.[102] Netease also signed an agreement in December 2021 with Sanya city in the southern Chinese province of Hainan to establish a Netease Metaverse Industry Base to promote the development of Hainan's digital innovation in the culture and content space.[103] It should be expected that more similar agreements between tech companies and local governments centered on the metaverse concept will mushroom in China this year.

Another important company is Huawei. Despite its smartphone business and its chip design unit being pushed to the edge of the cliff by U.S. sanctions, the telecommunications giant is actively pursuing opportunities in the metaverse. Huawei released its first quasi-VR device back in 2016, and unveiled its first VR glasses, Huawei VR Glass, in 2019. Chinese media reports estimated that around 300,000 units of Huawei VR Glass were sold as of October 2020, not an impressive amount by Huawei's scale. The company reportedly was incurring losses because the price for the product was set roughly at cost.[104]

There are conflicting rumors about Huawei's plans for future VR products. Some suggested that Huawei may discontinue its VR product, while others are expecting that the company may launch a second-generation VR device.[105] Overall consumer feedback on Huawei's VR product has been average, with most viewing the product as not being particularly competitive. Different from Meta's Oculus and other VR headsets, Huawei's VR glasses are used to primarily watch content and don't provide good and immersive experiences for playing VR games.

Besides hardware, Huawei is attempting to create a metaverse ecosystem that encompasses semiconductors and platforms. Huawei released its XR chips designed by its semiconductor unit HiSilicon in 2020. The XR chip incorporates HiSilicon's own NPU (neural processing unit) framework. Huawei is hoping to position its Harmony Operating System (OS) as the operating system for China's metaverse. It has partnered with a Chinese gaming company to better deliver metaverse games in the age of 5G. Huawei released a phone-based AR platform called Cyberverse in 2019 that merges the virtual and physical world in a wide array of applications. In 2021, Huawei released an app based on Cyberverse to allow users to experience virtual worlds superimposed on their real environment.

In terms of tools, Huawei released an end-to-end solution helping improve the efficiency of 3D VR content production. Huawei houses its own AREngine, an augmented reality engine, that works with its Cybervese technology to easily integrate the virtual world with the real world for developers.[106]

For XR hardware, Taiwanese company HTC Corporation is a noteworthy company with a more established market position than other Chinese device makers. It released its first VR headset in 2016 and has been one of the top-selling devices in the market. In 2020, it had a market share of 16.27% among VR users on Steam[107], which is a game distribution service by American video game developer Valve. But HTC's market share has been squeezed since 2021 by newer products such as Oculus. As of February 2022, HTC's Vive headset had only a 7.27% share on Steam.[108]

HTC has ambitions beyond hardware. In March, it announced Viverse, an open and accessible metaverse ecosystem that the company wants to help create. Viverse provides an array of tools, services, and platforms for people, companies, creators, and developers to "enrich a new immersive space."[109] A demo video shared by the company shows a user viewing health data floating in midair while running on a treadmill, or entering an immersive virtual world after putting on a VR headset.

"We really believe in the open Metaverse so that nobody or company should own/control it, and it should be accessible to as many people as possible," said Alvin Wang Graylin, China President at HTC. "What we are doing now is to deliver the enabling platforms, toolkits, and access devices that will allow more developers to create amazing content and users to enjoy superior immersive experiences." It sounds like an attractive vision, but how will HTC deliver that vision is less clear.

The Chinese metaverse space is following the footsteps of its American peers. At this stage, there is a big gap between Chinese companies and American companies in terms of advanced technology and commitment. From the semiconductors that power the metaverse to game engines and global platforms, American companies lead by a large margin.

In terms of human capital, Meta has more than 10,000 people working on the metaverse. The teams working on the metaverse/XR at Chinese tech companies are much smaller at hundreds of people on average but often much smaller. Some Chinese tech companies including Alibaba and Tencent have reduced the size of their R&D teams in XR a few years ago after the industry entered a phase of disillusionment. As Chinese tech companies are laying off thousands of employees this year amid the worst industry upheaval, the gap could even widen in headcount.

Looking ahead, Chinese companies are likely to excel in applications. China's metaverse industry will benefit from the country's massive market scale and companies' incredible speed in execution. This strikes a strong parallel to this author's previous book on China's artificial intelligence sector.

But this time, whether Chinese companies can innovate with their business models remains a question mark as Beijing seems determined to place the tech sector under tight government control. If the government decides to put the metaverse in similar positions as AI or big data, governments will again be a major client, backer, investor, and partner of the industry. But the space for Chinese companies' capabilities to innovate has shrunken significantly now, both when compared to two years ago in China and compared to international peers. There is more red tape, less space for new things, and uncertainty, while the reward for risk-taking has significantly diminished.

In addition, the regulatory and legal environment in China is very different from the West. For example, cryptocurrencies mining, trading, and exchanges are banned, and NFTs are not allowed to be traded on secondary markets in China. Some American companies' products such as Meta's Oculus and Google's AR glasses are likely not going to be available in China. China's tough crackdown on gaming and extracurricular education sectors means those sectors' evolution toward the metaverse will have a very different trajectory.

Despite all these uncertainties, one thing is for sure: the U.S. and China will be the twin gravitational centers in the future fantasy virtual world.

2.3. The Rest of the World

Other countries around the world are marching into the metaverse, and Asia, with its massive and successful gaming and entertainment industries, has a natural advantage adopting to the metaverse.

South Korea has been one of the most high-profile and deeply-committed countries announcing big plans. While China's central government has been relatively cautious and has not announced any official national-level campaigns so far, South Korea's Ministry for Science and ICT launched a collaborative partnership in 2021 with big local tech companies including SK Telecom and Hyundai Motor to develop metaverse platforms. South Korea also announced a Digital New Deal 2.0 that aims to develop an open metaverse platform and boost investments into areas such as blockchain and cloud.

The capital city, Seoul, plans to turn itself into the world's first metaverse city, where citizens can enjoy public services such as education, civil services, and tourism in the virtual world. In January 2022, the Korean Ministry of Science and ICT announced more specific blueprints to make South Korea the fifth-largest metaverse market globally (South Korea has the 10th largest GDP globally) by developing 220 metaverse firms and 40,000 industry experts by 2026.[110]

These initiatives are backed by government investments. For example, the government pledged to invest US$7.5 billion into digital technologies in 2022, with 9% devoted to the metaverse and cloud industries.[111] The city of Seoul is investing around US$3.2 billion in its Metaverse Seoul project to allow citizens to "meet with avatar officials" to deal with civic complaints and do much more in the virtual capital city.[112]

South Korea, being the world's fourth-largest gaming market (behind China, the U.S., and Japan)[113] and a major entertainment hotspot, is well-positioned in the migration to the metaverse. K-Pop fans are already familiar with virtual entertainment, with Korean stars having performed online during the Covid pandemic with as many as 756,000 attendees. South Korean entertainment companies such as Cube Entertainment is developing a K-Pop metaverse to host virtual concerts and allow fans to exchange NFTs (non-fungible token).

Samsung, the South Korean tech titan, is experimenting with metaverse applications. In January 2022, the company debuted a virtual store modeled on its flagship New York City location called Samsung 837X on Decentraland, a blockchain-powered virtual world. Visiting avatars can view Samsung company news in a theater and join a mixed reality dance party, among other things.

One month later, Samsung held a launch event for its new Galaxy smartphones inside 837X on Decentraland to allow more people to experience the event in the metaverse. But in a sign of how early and premature the metaverse is, many visitors were unable to join the event after frustratingly long waits when trying to log in.[114] Samsung also worked with 3D avatar and social app Zepeto to create a virtual home housing its products during the global electronics expo CES 2022 in the United States, indicating that the company is taking the metaverse seriously and developing its strategy via constant experimentation.

Of course, Samsung's Gear VR headset has been one of the more popular products in the market for years. Yet, the company hasn't released a new version of the headset since 2017 and there is currently no indication when the company might unveil updated VR headsets.

But the company has made a few moves in the AR space. It showcased how AR could be incorporated into a car's windshield to display data such as the weather, tire pressure, and maps during CES 2022. And previously, it showed off an AR glasses application use case designed for virtual workouts.

Leaked videos suggest that Samsung is working on a pair of AR glasses: one Lite version for consuming content in AR and another more elaborate one designed to work with potential holographic features.[115] It appears that consumers may not have too long a wait to try out Samsung AR glasses, as there are reports of the company already coordinating a release date. As a semiconductor manufacturing giant, Samsung's AR device will use its own advanced Exynos system-on-chips and use Google Android for its operating system. Samsung is also reportedly working with Microsoft to develop another AR headset.[116]

Japan is equally enthusiastic about the metaverse. One of the largest Japanese conglomerates, Sony, the maker of the best-selling gaming console of all time PlayStation, also sells the PlayStation VR headset, which is one of the most popular VR headsets in the market. In February 2022, the company released information about its next-generation PlayStation VR2, featuring a new sleeker design, state-of-art graphical rendering, enhanced tracking, and many other improved functions.[117]

Sony didn't announce when the new VR headset will be released, but it will certainly be a formidable contender in the global VR headset battlefield.

Like Google, Sony suffered a failed attempt in AR. It released smart glasses in 2015 but has discontinued the product due to poor reception. It's unclear if Sony is planning on resuscitating its AR ambitions.

Japan is the world's third-largest gaming market helmed by leading companies like Nintendo. The company's president Shuntaro Furukawa said that the metaverse has great potential and the company is studying how to approach the technology from a unique angle.[118] With its existing market position, the Japanese gaming industry will certainly be a major player in the metaverse gaming sector.

Another space that Japan is uniquely positioned is virtual idols. The country is home to some of the most successful virtual idols in the world. Hatsune Miku, a virtual idol and pop star (also called a vocaloid) released in 2007, tours around the world often with thousands of in-person concert-goers and hundreds of thousands more fans watching online live streaming.[119] During the concert, she is projected as a 3D hologram on a translucent screen on the stage to give a 3D imagery as if she is really there. As home to the distinctive visual art form, anime, Japanese companies have the capacity to create virtual idols with a global appeal that could become future cultural phenomena in the metaverse.

India is another country that is likely to play an important role in the future metaverse. Home to 440 million gamers and over half a trillion users for social media and e-commerce services, India has a massively scaled user base for the metaverse. Indian tech companies including Tata Consultancy Services, Infosys, HCL Technologies, and Wipro are developing various metaverse applications. The country's thriving startup scene is also witnessing the explosion of metaverse startups. It is estimated that almost 100,000 Indians are involved in metaverse projects.[120] India will predictably become an important player in both the production and consumption of metaverse applications.

As we have seen from previous sections, the tech landscape in the age of the metaverse will share some of the characteristics of the internet and mobile internet era. As such, Europe will likely continue to play an important role in pioneering regulation. Indeed, Margrethe Vestager, the executive vice president of the European Commission for A Europe Fit for the Digital Age, has expressed concerns for the regulatory implications of the metaverse.

"The metaverse will present new markets and a range of different businesses. There will be a marketplace where someone may have a dominant position," Vestager said, referring to potential antitrust implications.[121] She recognized that it is still early in the development of the metaverse, but Europe will be a critical entity in metaverse regulation.

Global tech companies will no doubt pay great attention to the European market, which boasts one of the largest groups of affluent consumers who can afford VR headsets. Meta, for example, said it plans to hire 10,000 people in the European Union over the next five years to help it build the metaverse.[122] Others like Google, Microsoft, and Apple have earlier announced plans to invest in data centers and digital transformations in Europe. Some of those are likely to cover metaverse development in the future.

China's Tencent has likewise increased investment in European game companies, while others like Huawei and ByteDance have big operations in the region as well. Europe will be a hotly contested market for American, Chinese, Korean, and Japanese companies to compete and penetrate their own metaverse ecosystems. But with likely a very strict regulatory environment, Europe will be a challenging market.

Chapter 3. Technology

3.1. XR Hardware: VR, AR, MR

Participants will have many ways to access the metaverse in the future: via phones, glasses, headsets, or other devices. But XR hardware will be the bridge to the most immersive and the best experiences.

There are currently three main types of hardware pertinent to the metaverse. A VR (virtual reality) headset, like Meta's Oculus Quest, Pico, and Sony's PlayStation VR, transfers the wearer into the immersive virtual world and disconnects them from the physical environment as the headset blocks all external vision. VR headsets are best used for consuming immersive content like VR games and VR content.

AR (augmented reality) and MR (mixed reality), viewed via a pair of glasses or goggles, or directly viewable from a phone and other devices, normally don't block the wearer's external vision. AR allows users to view the physical world that is "augmented" by computer-generated input such as graphics, video, sound, and other data. Pokémon Go is an accessible AR game that many people have played. MR is a hybrid reality, which merges the real and virtual worlds to allow physical and digital objects to co-exist and interact in real-time. Microsoft's Hololens is a type of MR device.

Smart glasses, like Ray-Ban Stories and Google Glass, normally project digital content in front of the user's eyes to provide a new hands-free way of interacting with information. XR, which stands for extended reality, is an umbrella term covering all the different types of real-and-virtual combined environment technologies. It should be noted that these definitions of devices and categories are rapidly evolving as technologies advance. The distinctions between each category are blurring and the format of devices is shifting. For example, AR is likely to be used on car windshields in the future and there are head-mounted AR devices without the glasses.

The XR market is expected to grow rapidly. Some expect the global XR market using a broad definition to grow at 85.2% in compound annual growth rate (CAGR) to reach US$160 billion by 2023.[123] Others predict the global XR market to reach US$393 billion by 2025 with a CAGR of 69.4%.[124] XR device shipments are expected to grow from 11 million in 2021 to 105 million in 2025.[125] Despite quite large differences in estimates, all researchers foresee robust growth rates over the next few years.

North America is currently the largest market in terms of revenue, but Asia-Pacific, led by China, has the fastest growth rate.[126] The consumer VR hardware and content market will be a major sub-market, which is forecasted to be worth US$16 billion by 2026, a 148% growth compared to 2021, according to a research firm Omdia.[127]

The competition for XR devices is already heated. There are many products in the market and more are in the pipeline. Meta currently has the most successful consumer VR headset, the US$299 Oculus Quest 2, which sold over 10 million headsets since its release in mid-2019.[128] The Oculus headset accounts for around 48% of the global install base, and is likely to increase to 50% by 2026, according to Omdia. Meta is also working on a more high-end standalone headset combining VR and AR codenamed Project Cambria, and consumer AR glasses codenamed Project Nazare. Meta is developing a haptic glove that will let users "feel" virtual objects. These products are expected to be unveiled to consumers in the coming years.

Meta is also researching more futuristic products, developing a wristband that translates motor signals from the brain to move virtual objects just by thinking about it.[129] Meta partnered with glasses maker Ray-Ban to release smart glasses called Ray-Ban Stories in 2021.

In the near future, Meta will boast a suite of XR hardware more comprehensive than its rivals. Partly due to the company's massive investments into the metaverse, Meta's shares have suffered since its big announcement last November. Whether this hardware will catch on with consumers will be key to the success of Meta's metaverse future.

Microsoft is more focused on enterprise applications and MR. Its US$3,500 Hololens MR smart glasses target enterprise usages. Equipped with hand and eye tracking, with spatial mapping and voice commands, Hololens allows wearers to interact with 3D digital objects using their hands or to reconstruct physical spaces virtually through the embedded software. The product has already found uses in the manufacturing, healthcare, and education sectors. Microsoft has reportedly sold tens of thousands of Hololens to companies like automakers and coffee machine makers. The U.S. military also signed a US$22 billion contract in 2021 for Microsoft to deliver over 120,000 custom-built headsets to the U.S. Army over 10 years.

Apple, the world's best consumer hardware company, is rumored to be planning to release a VR/AR headset as early as the end of 2022. It could be a VR, AR, or MR device. It could come with fancy features such as typing in the air with a virtual keyboard or sharpening part of the field of vision according to where users' eyes are looking (think of a camera that reads your mind placing the focus of the picture where your eyes are looking at while blurring the periphery).

Apple is also rumored to be releasing AR glasses offering optical see-through AR experience. The glasses will "bring information from your phone to your face," which can display data such as texts, emails, maps, and games over the user's field of vision by synchronizing with their iPhone. Apple's patent records suggest that its AR glasses could offer functions like a better vision in the dark, 3D maps, and holograms of virtual objects. Further out into the future, digital holograms could potentially replace all of the screens people use. Apple is reportedly working on this too, albeit at an experimental stage.

Google is one of the earliest tech companies to launch a mass-market AR product. Its AR smart glasses called Google Glass started selling to a select group of consumers in 2013, but the company was forced to stop the product rollout in 2015 amid privacy concerns. In 2017, Google Glass pivoted to focus on enterprise applications. Its Google Glass Enterprise Edition was deployed in factories to help workers read manuals and watch instructional videos via voice commands while working on certain components, for example. Since then, the enterprise product has been expanding its use cases to education, healthcare and other sectors, but there are no estimates on how sales are going.

Google appears to not have any plans to get into traditional VR devices for now. In 2021, Google unveiled Starline, an experimental video chat booth that allows users to see real-life 3D models of the other person with whom they are chatting. People sit in something like a photo selfie booth without the need of a headset and each party sees the other as if they are in the same room together. This thereby hits another technological roadmap milestone of an immersive experience without having to strap something on the head. Starline is currently only available in some Google offices, but the company plans to deploy the product with partners first in the healthcare and media sectors.

The Japanese company Sony is the maker of one of the most popular PlayStation VR headsets. In February 2022, the company released information about its next-generation PlayStation VR2, featuring a new sleek design, state-of-art graphical rendering, enhanced tracking, and many other improved functions without announcing the release date. After suffering a failed attempt to make it in AR, Sony hasn't publicly stated if it is planning to revive its AR product line.

South Korean tech giant Samsung is the maker of its Gear VR headset, one of the more popular VR products. Yet, the company hasn't released a new version of the headset since 2017 and there is currently no sign when the company might unveil updated VR headsets. But Samsung is displaying great interests in AR. It showcased how AR could be incorporated into a car's windshield to display data such as the weather, tire pressure, and maps during CES 2022. Previously, it showed off an AR glasses application use case designed for virtual workouts and smart glasses concept. Leaked videos also suggest that Samsung is working on a pair of AR glasses, one Lite version for consuming content in AR and another more elaborate one designed for the workplace with potential embedded holographic features.

HP's Reverb G2 VR headset, Valve Corporation's Valve Index VR headset, and the Vive VR headset are some other major contenders in this market. But some of these companies, including Oculus and Google, currently do not have their products available and are unlikely to become available in the Chinese market, where competition for the XR hardware market is heating up too.

ByteDance, the owner of the short video app TikTok, acquired a VR headset maker called Pico in August 2021. Pico was the third-largest virtual reality headset maker globally in the first quarter of 2021[130], and claims to have 58% of the Chinese VR device market in the fourth quarter of 2020 (these rankings change rapidly).[131] The acquisition gave ByteDance an instant lead in market share in China. Even though Pico's sales are much smaller at around half a million in cumulative shipments, it could grow rapidly.

Tencent is rumored to be in deal talks with a number of VR headset makers, including Taiwanese electronics firm HTC, Chinese video platform iQiyi (both have VR headset units), and an independent headset maker Dapeng VR to potentially get into XR devices. Among them, Dapeng VR is an independent VR headset maker in China founded in 2015, and it was ranked as the second biggest company during the first quarter of 2021 in this space. [132] Having raised around US$10 million in financing in 2021, Dapeng is a ripe acquisition target.

Tencent reportedly also bought a niche game phone maker called Black Shark Corporation in January 2022. Black Shark's phones are customized for playing mobile games. But its hardware expertise could be useful if Tencent decides to launch its own XR device. Black Shark is reportedly tasked with developing a VR headset for Tencent after the acquisition.

Alibaba has invested in American AR startup Magic Leap, and has recently invested in a Chinese AR glasses maker. In addition, Alibaba established a new company in August 2021 with its businesses covering VR equipment, indicating that the e-commerce giant may be entering into XR hardware as well.

Huawei released its first quasi-VR device back in 2016, and unveiled its first VR glass, Huawei VR Glass, in 2019. Chinese media reports estimated that around 300,000 units of Huawei VR Glass were sold as of October 2020, which is not an impressive amount by Huawei's scale. The company reportedly was incurring losses because the price for the product was set roughly at cost.[133]

There are conflicting rumors about Huawei's plans for future VR products. Some suggested that Huawei may discontinue its VR product, while others were expecting that the company may launch a second-generation VR device.[134] Overall consumer feedback on Huawei's VR product has been average, with most viewing the product as not being particularly competitive. Different from Meta's Oculus and other VR headsets, Huawei's VR glasses are used to primarily watch content and don't provide good experiences for playing VR games. It's worth watching if Huawei will release any updated and more competitive XR devices.

Taiwanese company HTC Corporation has a more established market position than other Chinese device makers.

It released its first VR headset in 2016 and has been one of the top-selling devices in the market. In 2020, it had a market share of 16.27% among VR users on Steam[135], which is a game distribution service by American video game developer Valve. But HTC's market share has been squeezed since 2021 by newer products such as Oculus. As of February 2022, HTC's Vive headset had only a 7.27% share on Steam.[136]

It's important to note that most of the VR hardware makers rely on American chips and OS. The VR supply chain is similar to that of smartphones. VR device makers used Qualcomm mobile chips previously, but since Qualcomm released an XR-specific chip, Snapdragon XR2, it has become the most competitive chip in the market. Oculus Quest 2, Pico Neo 3, and iQUT 3 (the VR headset made by Chinese video platform iQiyi) all use Qualcomm Snapdragon XR2 chips because of its advanced capabilities and performance.

Huawei's chip unit HiSilicon released an XR chip in 2020. It was used to power an AR glasses product by Chinese company Rokid in a showcase.[137] But this chip is likely no longer manufactured due to U.S. sanctions. Some smaller Chinese chip companies such as Rockchip and Allwinner Technology are designing VR chips. It is likely that some low- and medium-end VR devices powered by Chinese-designed VR chips will be released in the near future[138], but the technology gap will remain significant. Chinese-designed chips won't be able to compete with Qualcomm's high-end chips any time soon.

In terms of operating systems (OS), Android is the dominant OS for VR devices. Most of the VR devices use the Android OS, or use a modified OS based on Android. A small number of device makers use Windows as their OS. Most AR device makers are also based on Android. Some companies are developing their own OS: Microsoft's Hololens uses an OS based on Windows and Magic Leap developed its own OS, Lumin OS. Similarly, AR products mostly use Qualcomm Snapdragon chips and there are currently no custom-designed chips for AR. Nevertheless, the Android/Qualcomm ecosystem ruling the mobile phone market is likely going to become the de facto setup for XR devices.

Optics is another critical component for XR devices and accounts for a large portion of the costs. It appears that American tech companies are diversifying their supplier base. Apple and Meta have both made investments into various optics manufacturers. Oculus has added Japanese companies like Sony as optical display suppliers to its VR headset, after relying on Chinese company BOE Technology as a major supplier initially, according to an insider who is not optimistic that Chinese suppliers will play any important roles in the upstream XR supply chain for global tech giants.

But Chinese companies have historically been strong in serving as original equipment manufacturers (OEM). Goertek Inc., which started out as an acoustic components company, has become a major OEM for the world's largest XR makers. Goertek makes the Oculus Quest 2 VR headset for Meta, and is manufacturing VR headsets for most of the top XR device makers including Sony, HTC, and Pico.[139]

The XR industrial supply chain shares many familiar characteristics with other tech sectors, whereby American companies hold key advantages in advanced technology and

Chinese companies heavily rely on core foreign parts. This market condition will likely take a long time to change.

3.2. Game Engines

A game engine is software designed to develop video games, usually with a 2D or 3D rendering engine. Its usage goes beyond creating video games to applications like data visualization and digital twin creations, and is therefore important to the creation of the metaverse.

Similar to how the video sharing site, YouTube, operates, the metaverse will rely on user-generated-content, because it's unrealistic for one or a few entities to create limitless virtual experiences. Like how video editing software iMovie and Final Cut Pro help consumers create YouTube content, game engines provide the critical tool that allows regular users to create their own virtual spaces.

The game engine market itself is not big in terms of revenue. The global game engines market is expected to reach US$3.6 billion by the end of 2024, growing at a CAGR of 13% between 2019 to 2024, according to one estimate.[140] But it plays a core function, and is where the U.S. and Chinese markets have vastly different characteristics.

American companies are the dominant players on the global stage. Unity Technologies' Unity game engine and Epic Games' Unreal Engine have a 48% and 13% global market share, respectively. More than half of all mobile games are built in Unity and more than 60% to 70% of everything built for VR or AR or XR are built in Unity, the company's CEO John Riccitiello said in 2018.[141] Millions of game developers start about 150,000 new projects each day in Unity, which also conveniently supports over 25 platforms such as iOS, Windows Mixed Reality, Android TV, and PS4.

These two companies also have the most advanced technology and the largest ecosystem after decades of operation. A game engine provides functionalities including rendering, physics engine, animation, artificial intelligence, streaming, localization, and many other features. Unity and Unreal engine, first released in 2005 and 1998 respectively, grew up together and defined the game engine industry. Today, publicly-listed Unity is valued at US$26 billion and Epic Games (which owns Unreal Engine) is valued at US$17.3 billion.[142]

Epic Games' Unreal Engine powers immensely popular games such as Fortnite with 80 million monthly active users. It also has evolved through different iterations to the latest Unreal Engine 5, which will be fully released in early 2022. The scenes generated by Unreal Engine are so realistic and powerful that it has been used in the film, animation, and architecture industries. Unity is used by these industries too.

The film The Mandalorian used Unreal Engine to build entire 3D environments on the set. Movie crews don't have to recreate physical war zones, for example, and can use digital backgrounds generated by Unreal Engine. The scenes are displayed on screens and can synchronize the lighting in the virtual background with the lighting in the physical movie set. It creates an innovative and convenient way for filmmaking at a fraction of the costs.

Game engines can also be used to create digital twins, which are virtual presentations of a physical object or process. An example is a digital twin of a factory that has many useful applications, like the previously-mentioned digital twin of a BMW factory created by Nvidia that helps reduce costs for the car company.

Other game engines in the U.S. include Amazon Lumberyard and CryEngine. A new player in the space is Nvidia, an American chip design giant known for its GPU processors. The company unveiled Omniverse, a one-stop destination for developers and creators to access not only Nvidia's own tools, but also third-party tools. Ominverse aims to incorporate as many third-party tools onto Omniverse as possible and to pool different ecosystems together. Currently, a developer creates one avatar in Unreal Engine and may not be able to use that avatar in a different game engine. Omniverse attempts to solve that problem by attracting all the major creation tools to participate in its ecosystem.

Unity has a dominant position in China, with more than 60% of the market share in the country. Around 15% of Unity's revenue comes from China. Even though Chinese users have the highest engagement globally, monetization levels have been low in China,[143] due to rampant usage of pirate software. Unity's China chief said in 2020 that pirate Unity software users in China take account for 80% of all of the company's global pirate software users. The company has used legal measures, such as sending attorney letters, to combat pirate software. It is also moving certain functions to the cloud to reduce pirate software usage, but the progress is slow.[144]

China doesn't have powerful game engine companies like Unity and Unreal Engine. Even though Tencent owns 40% of Epic Games, U.S. regulators are looking into national security risks relating to Tencent's ownership. Tencent may be forced to sell its stakes in Epic Games or make certain arrangements to address regulators' security concerns.

One major reason why there haven't been any powerful game engine companies in China is because the commercial environment and user habit of paying for licensed software are still not yet widely established in China. Another reason is that Chinese game engines are latecomers, and game engines require a long-term dedicated commitment to technology and ecosystem build-up.

China's most successful open-source game engine, Chukong Technologies' Cocos, started in 2010, later than its American peers. Moreover, the research of computer graphics and 3D real-time graphics in China began much later. Aside from a lack of talent, China's game engine market faces added pressure because it is not an easy standalone business. Market leader Unity still hasn't been able to make a profit yet. Unreal Engine is free to use and only charges 5% of revenues for those games that make over US$1 million in lifetime gross revenues.

These factors influence each other. Because developing game engines doesn't make money, particularly so in China, there are not a lot of career opportunities and hence fewer students are willing to learn the relevant skills. Because users are not willing to pay for licensed software, it's much harder for game engine operators to make enough revenues to survive. Cocos is open source and free to use. It makes money from derivative services such as training and ads. All of these are challenges for any company trying to build a successful game engine.

Cocos game engine is able to carve a niche market for itself. It is popular among 2D mobile game developers in Asia, and small and leisure games in the overseas market. Cocos has registered developers of over 1.4 million and powers over 100,000 games in the app stores.[145] It also has a 53% market share in China's small games market.[146] It doesn't compete directly with Unity and Unreal Engine, which caters to more complicated, 3D game development.

Cocos is trying to expand its appeal. In 2021, it added an all-in-one 3D engine and editor to its game engine, allowing developers to develop 3D games.[147] But the gap between Cocos and its American peers is vast. From a technology perspective, Cocos would not be able to do what Unreal Engine can do in rendering and graphics for a long while, or maybe ever. The company's CEO has said that Cocos does not plan to pursue high-end applications for the engine like in films and entertainment. Instead, Cocos will focus on real-time rendering that is lightweight and more flexible and used in computing power-constrained environments such as on mobile and small terminal devices.[148]

Given that the game engine community is highly sticky (a developer who learned and used Unity for years is incentivized to stay within Unity), Cocos will likely remain a niche market segment leader. The company is paying close attention to the metaverse but the CEO has not disclosed any other actions the company may take.

Lastly, many big gaming companies have their own self-developed game engines. Activision Blizzard, Electronic Arts, Take-Two Interactive, Ubisoft, and Tencent all have in-house game engines. For these large-scale game development teams, it makes more sense to hire a few programmers to develop an internal game engine, renderer, and tools customized to meet their needs and to save on licensing fees at the same time.

Unity and Unreal Engine are likely to keep their market duopoly for a long time and lead the industry in the technology frontier. The American pair will likely dominate the Chinese market as well. And so, the metaverse will largely be built with game engines made by American companies.

3.3. Virtual Humans & Avatars

The metaverse needs virtual environments that can be explored and enjoyed by people. As a core ingredient of the metaverse, virtual humans are the prerequisite for applications within games, social networking, and virtual work. The first step a newly-registered participant takes in any metaverse platform from Second Life to Horizon Worlds is to create their own virtual identity, and consumers view the ability to choose their avatar's physical appearance as a key feature in terms of overall enjoyment within the metaverse.[149]

Like other elements of the metaverse, virtual humans are nothing new. The use of computer graphics, motion capture, artificial intelligence, and other methods to create digital images of people and avatars has existed for decades. A wide array of virtual idols, avatars, and virtual assistants have been used in industries from films, games, customer service to standup comedy. With technologies advancing over the years, particularly artificial intelligence, 3D modeling, and computer graphics, it has become easier and faster to create virtual humans with highly realistic details. The line between real and fake is rapidly blurring.

There are two technical paths for the generation of virtual humans. The first is 3D computer graphics modeling. This is used to make a 1:1 restoration of the appearance, expressions, and actions of a real person. This method is prohibitively expensive and also does not capture high-quality photo-realistic color.[150] The second is artificial intelligence-based automatic modeling. Skipping the 3D whole-body sensing part of the process, this method greatly reduces the costs and simplifies the process of virtual human production. Sometimes, these two methods are combined to create virtual humans.

The bar for virtual human creation has steadily lowered and this capability is becoming more widely available. Unreal Engine, for example, unveiled a cloud-based app in 2021 called MetaHuman Creator for anyone to make high-fidelity virtual humans. It cuts virtual human creation time from weeks or months to less than an hour, while delivering the same high-quality results and details. Videos of sample virtual humans released by MetaHuman Creator show digital replicas that are hard to distinguish from real humans.[151]

Similarly, Nvidia's Omniverse platform provides avatar generation functions with the focus on creating AI assistants for industries from restaurant orders to bank transactions. Unity's game engine, as well as Unreal Engine and Omniverse, are offering virtual human creation tools as extra benefits for attracting users to use their game engines. These big game engines are leaders in the rendering and modeling of virtual humans with unparalleled technological sophistication. There are many niche players in the market, such as Soul-Machine, Oben, Loom.ai, VICON, Opti Track, and Xsens, each with different focuses in technology and business approach.

The Chinese equivalent to Unreal Engine/Unity/Omniverse may be Xiaoice, which was originally a chatbot project incubated inside Microsoft in 2014 and spun off as an independent company in 2020. Xiaoice began as a text chatbot, evolved to voice conversations, then to being a virtual human creation platform.

Xiaoice, in which Microsoft still owns an unspecified stake, utilizes an AI-based virtual person generation platform to help enterprises rollout customized virtual characters equipped with language capabilities tailored to specific industries. These virtual persons have served as virtual news anchors, virtual fashion designers, virtual idols, virtual teachers, and virtual financial accountants.

Virtual humans created by Xiaoice are used by major companies in China from China Unicom, BMW, and Nissan. Xiaoice also has strong positions in the Japanese and Indonesian markets. Customer inquiries are booming as more enterprises want to create their own virtual assistants or other types of virtual employees. By the company's estimates, it has generated tens of millions of AI beings (some beings may not necessarily take the form of humans), and the company raised venture funding in 2021 that valued it at over US$1 billion.[152] It seems that no American independent virtual human companies have attained this unicorn valuation.

Xiaoice's virtual humans are not as high fidelity with high versatility as those generated by Omniverse and Unreal Engine, but it is very strong in scaling up user applications. This seems to reinforce the existing respective technological strengths of the U.S., which is strong in advanced tech, and China, which is strong in applications.

This distinction extends to the entire Chinese virtual human market, which generally has a much larger scale and deeper penetration. Virtual hosts for e-commerce live streaming, for example, have been rapidly adopted in China. Virtual hosts are the fastest-growing category on the Chinese live-streaming portal Bilibili. Subscriptions and tips to virtual idols on Bilibili increased 350% in 2020.[153] The Chinese virtual idol market is expected to grow at 70% in 2021[154] and the potential consumers of virtual idols stand at over 400 million.[155]

Moreover, there are dozens of smaller Chinese companies whose focus is on virtual human businesses aimed at specific use cases and serving the needs of enterprises. Some of these companies rely on Unreal Engine's MetaHuman Creator to generate the virtual humans, then spend most of the energy creating a personal story, intensive marketing campaigns, and user engagement. The virtual idols make money by serving enterprise clients as brand ambassadors or to promote e-commerce sales.

This business model seems to work well only for the top companies that can successfully create a virtual celebrity. It's unclear how many of these application-focused companies can grow into sustainable business models, because the technology barrier is relatively low and the use cases are highly segmented. Indeed, several virtual idol companies have failed.

South Korea and Japan are strong players in virtual humans too. Korean tech giant Samsung showcased its strong technology by introducing Neon, an AI-powered virtual human that is indistinguishable from real people, during CES 2020.[156] Demo videos of Neon are equally jaw-dropping, showing characters from a Yoga instructor to a banker, that are truly life-like with hyper-realistic facial expressions and body gestures.

Samsung didn't say much about how and where Neon will be applied, except that Neon could be people's future virtual life companions, a vague term that is hard to define. But given Samsung's ecosystem, it's easy to imagine that Neon could be used as virtual assistants or friends on its many terminal devices, or to generate realistic humans for potential work-related metaverse applications.

Virtual idols have achieved great success in South Korea and Japan. K-Pop fans are already familiar with virtual entertainment, with Korean stars having performed online during the Covid pandemic with as many as 756,000 attendees. Companies are evolving into the metaverse quickly, with South Korean entertainment company Cube Entertainment developing a K-Pop metaverse to host virtual concerts allowing fans to exchange NFTs.

Japan is home to some of the most successful virtual idols in the world. Hatsune Miku, a virtual idol and pop star (also called a vocaloid) released back in 2007, tours around the world often with thousands of in-person concert-goers and hundreds of thousands more fans watching online live streaming.[157] During the concert, she is projected as a 3D hologram on a translucent screen on the stage to give 3D imagery as if she is really there performing for the masses.

In summary, American companies have the most advanced virtual human technology, as part of their overall impressive technology stack in game engines, 3D modeling, rendering, and computer graphics. They will continue blurring the line between real and fake. Chinese companies have pushed the boundaries of practical use cases of virtual humans, deployed the technology rapidly and broadly. And they may lead in how this technology can create real business value. Meanwhile, Korean and Japanese companies have their respective unique pop culture characteristics that will make them critical players for how virtual humans can enrich the metaverse experiences.

3.4. Blockchain, Decentralization, and NFTs

Some people have been calling for the metaverse to be based on blockchain technology, to be decentralized, and to rely on NFTs (non-fungible tokens) for value exchanges. These ideas are related to the Web3, a conceptualized new iteration of the World Wide Web based on blockchain technology incorporating features such as decentralization and token-based economics. Web3 will supposedly give users more data security and privacy, countering the influence of big tech companies that dominate Web 2.0. Similarly, some people argue, the metaverse should adopt this concept to give more control to the users and avoid the virtual world from being dominated by big tech.

These technologies may have a role to play in the metaverse, but this author believes that such a role will be either marginal or minor. The first chapter illustrated how big tech companies are building their metaverse in a fashion akin to adding an additional floor to an existing house, i.e., stacking the metaverse on their mobile internet ecosystem. Future regulatory and legal changes may force these companies to open up their closed ecosystems or enhance interoperability to a certain degree, but it will be a long rocky road to an uncertain outlook. Either way, it's difficult to picture complete breakups or the dissolution of large tech platforms.

Moreover, blockchain applications will be vastly different across different countries due to regulation. Cryptocurrency trading and mining are banned, and NFTs are not allowed to trade in the secondary market in China. Cryptocurrency is legal and treated in some countries (Australia, Japan) as property, but not in most places. There are no established legal frameworks on how to treat NTFs currently. When regulation is drawn, they will likely be as complicated as the intricate legal landscape for cryptocurrency. Therefore, how blockchain will shape the metaverse is likely going to fall on a wide spectrum of possibilities.

The most high-profile and successful blockchain-based decentralized metaverse projects are Decentraland and The Sandbox. Decentraland is a 3D virtual world platform where users can socialize, play and buy virtual plots of land. The platform is based on the Ethereum blockchain and completed an initial coin offering (ICO) in 2017, raising US$24 million. Today, Decentraland's token MANA boasts a total market capitalization of US$4.5 billion after a huge surge after the metaverse hype in the fall of 2021.[158] As of December 2021, Decentraland had around 300,000 monthly active users – notably similar to that of Meta's Horizon Worlds - and maximum concurrent users of 2,500.[159]

The Sandbox is another Ethereum-based virtual world where users create, build and sell digital assets in the so-called play-to-earn game model. It held an ICO in 2020, raising US$3 million. As of March 8, 2022, the market capitalization of its token SAND is around US$3.2 billion.[160] The company reportedly had 2 million total users, 19,000 land-owning users, and many thousands of artists working to create worlds on those lands.[161] In November 2021, the company claimed it had 30,000 monthly active users.[162]

Not only do their operations and market metrics stand out, but these two platforms have caught the imagination of the public and cemented their virtual worlds as the partner for top global companies. Many Fortune 500 companies including JPMorgan Chase and Samsung have set up virtual spaces inside Decentraland. Celebrities like Snoop Dogg and brands like The Walking Dead own land in The Sandbox.

Other notable projects include Axie Infinity, a popular NFT pet game; and Gala, a blockchain gaming platform. Enjin, High Street, Somnium Space, Meta Hero, Red Fox Labs, Bloktopia, Star Atlas, MetaCity, Theta Network, and Ultra are also competing in the same vibrant blockchain-based metaverse space.

One key challenge for these projects is the lack of interoperability. Similar to the crypto ecosystem, each of these blockchain-based metaverse projects has its own technical architecture, rules, virtual goods, and tokens. There is little interoperability among all the projects, which remain largely isolated and self-contained. If there are no efforts to build interoperability, virtual goods such as avatar clothing and tokens cannot freely move among different virtual worlds, and this will greatly limit user experience. This is an extremely hard problem to solve. Whether interoperability can be achieved will determine to a large degree how important a role blockchain-based metaverse will play in the future virtual worlds.

In China, the picture is entirely different. Because ICOs and crypto trading are banned, it's impossible to issue tokens and therefore use them as a means of value exchange. The most well-known "metaverse" project is called Honnverse, a 3D virtual world where users can socialize and trade digital assets. Launched by Chinese internet influencer manager company, Inmyshow Digital, Honnverse claims to build immersive virtual world experiences based on blockchain technology, allowing users to trade land and other digital assets based on NTFs. The publicly-listed Inmyshow Digital saw its share price jump 85.58% in 22 trading days following its Honnverse project was reported by the media in October 2021.[163]

But the ensuing chaotic frenzy about Honnverse was surprising to even its creators. When users were allowed to join the beta version of Honnverse, a mobile app that is not based on any blockchain and without any embedded NFTs initially, speculative trading went out of hand. With over 100,000 eager users flooding to the mobile app vying for a piece of virtual land inside Honnverse, prices skyrocketed by hundreds of times in one day. Many WeChat groups and QQ groups were formed as an unsupervised marketplace to match buyers and sellers. Some virtual land was listed on e-commerce platforms like Alibaba for sell.

Because Honnverse is not based on the blockchain initially and doesn't have its own tokens, trading of its virtual land took place in a highly risky manner. Users would add each other inside the Honnverse app as friends, then arrange trades among themselves in QQ or Wechat groups. Once both parties agreed on the price, they would transfer funds using third-party payment options like Alipay or WeChat Pay. Because these transactions take place outside of the app, there was no escrow mechanism to protect the buyers or sellers from fraud.

Eager traders of Honnverse virtual land were attracted by the fact that Honnverse is the Chinese version of Decentraland and The Sandbox. But there is nothing in common in their technology infrastructure. Not based on the blockchain and without any tokens, Honnverse lacks the transparency, immutability, traceability of transactions, trust mechanisms, and decentralized features of Decentraland and The Sandbox. It is just a mobile app dressed up to look like them. In true Dutch tulip bubble fashion, Honnverse virtual land prices collapsed after Chinese government authorities warned risks relating to virtual land speculation.[164]

In February 2022, the Honnverse operator told Chinese media that its virtual world will be based on Blockchain-based Service Network (BSN), a Chinese government-sanctioned blockchain framework founded by the State Information Center, China Mobile, and UnionPay, in the future. It indicates that the

Honnverse developer is still working on bringing a blockchain-based metaverse to market in a more compliant manner.

Consistent with government policy tendencies, Honnverse is exploring ways to make its metaverse valuable to the real economy. It partnered with Chateau Lafite Rochschild to promote sales of the high-end wine inside its virtual world. It collaborated with Chinese real estate developers to allow potential buyers to view and tour real houses inside its metaverse.[165]

But without its own token, it remains questionable how Honnverse users will be able to trade their digital goods. The answer may be some kind of government-backed digital currency like the e-CNY, a Central Bank Digital Currency (CBDC) devised by China's central bank.

The e-CNY is currently in trial operations in select cities and has been installed on many big tech platforms including JD.com, Meituan, Tmall, and Didi as payment options. As of the end of 2021, a total of 261 million e-CNY persona wallets have been established with a total recorded transaction value of over RMB87.6 billion (US$13.87 billion).[166] Compared to WeChat Pay's daily transaction value of RMB170 billion (US$27 billion), e-CNY's mass adoption still has a ways to go.

On the other hand, NFTs, which are usually referred to as "digital collections" in China and considered by some to be an important conduit for blockchain-based metaverse transactions, face a number of constraints in China. Chinese NFTs issuance usually has a small, limited quantity, making them more akin to rare digital collections. The categories are generally digital art, digital music, or digital trendy items. Most NFT platforms do not allow secondary market transactions so as to curb speculative trading. Buyers of NFTs are allowed only to transfer their digital collection to other people for free, or sometimes not even allowed to make any transfers at all. It can be argued that NFTs in China are not real NFTs as they lack the core features of decentralization, proof of ownership and free exchanges.

The Chinese NFTs market operates in perhaps the strictest regulatory environment. Regulators have cracked down on all activities related to cryptocurrencies, such as mining, initial coin offerings, trading and exchanges. NFTs are different from cryptocurrencies, but they share some characteristics. Both are based on blockchain, both are prone to speculative trading, and some NFTs require cryptocurrencies to trade. Therefore, companies who have issued NFTs including Tencent, JD.com, and Alibaba, are all very cautious to avoid hitting any regulator red lines.

For the U.S. and other countries where cryptocurrencies are legal, blockchain-based metaverses provide decentralized platforms and are facilitated by transactions based on cryptocurrencies and NFTs. These markets are likely to continue displaying a high level of volatility. Moreover, the tendency of cryptocurrencies increasingly being held by a small number of entities (top 0.01% of Bitcoin holders control 27% of the digital currency vs. the top 1% control 30% of total U.S. household wealth)[167] challenges its vision of decentralization.

The development of NFTs in China will likely proceed with a focus on compliance and strict regulation. "China will on one hand combat illegal and criminal behaviors and high-risk behaviors, and on the other hand promote the ability of independent innovation of core technologies," said Yang Dong, executive dean of the Blockchain Research Institute of Renmin University. "I believe that after this round of cleanup, China will not lag behind in the development of NFT and metaverse."[168]

Having an independent and self-controlled blockchain ecosystem has been a priority for Chinese policymakers. Tech platforms and state-owned-enterprises will take more responsibility for maintaining a healthy ecosystem, which will largely be centralized. The infrastructure will be mainly government-led and incorporate government-backed blockchain and government-backed digital currencies.

Chapter 4. Opportunities: How to Make It in the Metaverse

The metaverse will provide massive opportunities not only for big tech companies, but also for startups, career professionals, and investors. JPMorgan has predicted that the market opportunity in the metaverse could be worth a trillion dollars annually in the next couple of years[169], Goldman Sachs is putting the future worth of the global metaverse at US$8 trillion, while Morgan Stanley makes the most jaw-dropping outlook of US$8 trillion for China's metaverse opportunity alone.[170]

The previous chapters show that the largest opportunities may be enjoyed by big tech companies. But there is still a wide range of potential areas that companies and investors of all sizes and startup teams can take advantage of. The metaverse is the next iteration of the internet, therefore it covers a wide range of sectors from infrastructure, hardware, tools, platforms, and content. Horizontally, it has applications in almost all industries, such as social networking, games, healthcare, education, and manufacturing. Therefore, the metaverse opportunity is comparable to the internet opportunity in breadth and depth.

Metaverse's tech infrastructure includes things like 5G, semiconductors, cloud computing, and edge computing. While 5G and cloud computing require massive investment and resources, there are emergent niche markets in semiconductors, especially in China where the demand for domestically-designed chips is high. Most of the XR hardware on the market is powered by chips designed by U.S.-based Qualcomm or other chip giants, but some Chinese device makers have strong interests in experimenting with domestically-created chips to achieve more self-reliance and a diversified supplier network. A number of semiconductor companies are creating XR-tailored chips, and the number is expected to continue to grow in future decades.

The hardware and tools space is already very crowded with big tech companies and other competitors, but some investors are convinced that there are still opportunities for new entrants. A new VR company called Arpara is trying to win users with its unique features of 5K micro-OLED screens that are different from the industry standard of the 4K LCD screen used in Oculus Quest 2 (it is nearly 4K) and Pico Neo 3. The company has recently secured a round of angel investment.[171]

Another Chinese startup called Huiye Technology provides what it calls "AI-being-As-A-Service" to enterprises wanting to create their own virtual humans. Huiye's artificial intelligence-driven platform can automatically generate capabilities of virtual humans' movements and gestures based on music input, or automatically generate the correct mouth movements based on text or audio input. It has also received venture backing to scale up its go-to-market strategy.[172] Similar types of tools and software platforms helping metaverse projects deliver faster and more efficiently should be in high demand.

The biggest opportunity exists in content and applications. This is where most venture capital investments are made in China, at least. Among the dozens of investments into metaverse startups since 2021, a majority are related to content creations (which overlap with tools sometimes), virtual humans, and specific applications like games and social networking.

A number of companies own and operate virtual intellectual property content and virtual idols, including Next Generation, StarHeir Technology, i-Reality, and Ayayi. Many others provide tools to facilitate content creation. Versetech is a virtual space SaaS platform that helps enterprises generate their desired virtual worlds more efficiently. Banrenmao produces super-realistic and interactive digital content to be used in the metaverse. Similarly, HaiHuman Technology is a digital human technology company that makes this task easier for enterprises.

Other promising areas for startup teams and companies interested in expanding their businesses to the metaverse are vertical applications. Each new iteration of the internet has brought new platforms to life, such as Yahoo! and Google during the dot com era; and Uber and Lyft during the mobile internet era. The metaverse is likely to do the same. There are some clear early winners already, such as Roblox, Decentraland, and The Sandbox. But it is still very early and the market is wide open for new players.

In China, this is among the categories that investors have betted the most on. Vyou is a virtual social networking platform for players shown as cartoon characters. Burning Galaxy is a virtual game social platform. BUD is a 3D internet content social user-generated-content (UGC) platform. The race to become the next Roblox, or the Roblox of China/Japan/South Korea/Indonesia, is intensifying. To stand out in this competitive market, product developers must have distinct features, styles, or cultural elements that can resonate with targeted users.

There are many other market verticals ripe for new companies to create products, tools, and platforms for metaverse applications to flourish. Marketing and advertising will be a huge opportunity. Similar to how social media giants today have an ads-based business model, the metaverse will become an important destination for advertising spending as users migrate to the 3D internet. In-game ad spending is set to reach US$18.41 billion by 2027, according to one estimate.[173] Companies creating tools helping advertisers to better place and target their ads, or tools helping them create the best metaverse ads would find ample willing clients.

Likewise, business applications present strong use cases that can create real value and therefore a solid business model. Using digital twins, BMW has reduced production planning time by 30% in areas like simulating work order instructions for factory workers in the digital factory.[174] Ericsson is adopting digital twins to help determine how to construct 5G networks by simulating signal transmission through barriers. Siemens Energy estimates that digital twins can help it reduce downtime by 10% in the power plants it builds and services by simulating pipe corrosions.[175] The use of digital twins can also be applied in urban planning, which is expected to yield US$280 billion in cost savings by 2030.[176] These are large addressable markets, and companies who can help smooth the application scaling-up process will be much needed.

Education is another big use case. The internet and the mobile internet have nurtured many online education companies and educational mobile apps that were successful businesses. Before China's crackdown on its extra-curriculum education sector, China boasted the highest number of education unicorn companies (those with a valuation of US$1 billion). The metaverse will disrupt the education sector, with 3D immersive teaching and training providing better results and more enjoyable learning experiences. This market is currently almost a clean slate for new entrants to build the products, tools, and platforms to improve the educational experience, especially if remote learning becomes more common and accepted even after the pandemic.

The average company in the U.S. spent US$1,071 per employee in 2021 on training costs.[177] This training can be done with the help of VR or AR, which can significantly reduce training costs for companies. Markets like China will present unique challenges because of its crackdown on extra-curriculum education, but professional training services such as those for factory workers, technical jobs, medical students, architecture, and construction jobs still make up large and attractive opportunities.

Similarly, e-commerce will be transformed into 3D-commerce. Users will be able to see how a piece of clothing, or a pair of earrings or glasses will look on their bodies in 3D-commerce. They will be able to interact with goods in a 3D form virtually before making decisions to buy. This should greatly reduce the return ratio and therefore improve supply chain efficiencies. For retailers, they need to adopt the metaverse early and smartly to avoid being pushed to the side and seen as irrelevant. Some retailers failing to adopt e-commerce during the past 20 years have found themselves increasingly marginalized. This will replay again during the age of the metaverse.

And of course, games will be the starter and the main dish for the lavish metaverse banquets. Companies like Roblox that utilize user-generated-content to establish a metaverse platform and a creator economy represent a mature and proven business model. There is still plenty of space for new entrants in this segment. For high-end AAA game producers, they might need to supplement their high-quality, professionally-generated-content platforms to accommodate user-generated-content to retain users. Game companies like Take-Two, Activision Blizzard, and Sony with strong R&D capabilities and more open games ecosystems are likely to take full advantage of the metaverse opportunity. Blockchain-based game metaverse platforms with play-to-earn models should be able to attract an increasing number of users. The element of games could also be combined with education and 3D-commerce, for example, to generate enjoyable experiences and new businesses models.

For career professionals, the metaverse should be incorporated into their career planning. Any skills required for building the products, tools, and platforms of the metaverse will be in high demand in future decades. These include computer graphics, 3D modeling, rendering, game development using major game engines, artificial intelligence, optics technology that is critical to XR hardware, and virtual human creation.

The metaverse will likely nurture the next wave of leading technology companies, while at the same time push some existing ones to the sidelines. As a Chinese saying goes: one shall take action consistent with the natural evolution of things. Though there may be many risks and challenges in the metaverse, which we will review in the next chapter, no one can prevent its arrival. Those who make decisions consistent with the metaverse's evolution will find themselves in an advantageous position.

Chapter 5: Risks and Challenges

As with any new opportunity in business, there are many risks and challenges as we move toward the 3D internet. As governments around the world grapple with the big tech challenges such as misinformation, social division, anticompetitive behavior, and data privacy, companies should learn from past mistakes and address these risks before they build the metaverse. Because the future virtual world is more immersive, more emotionally involved, and may be accompanied by more invasive tracking, some of the challenges of the 2D internet could be compounded and therefore demand more preventive measures.

But before discussing the potential regulatory and ethical risks, it should be recognized that there are many technological challenges that need to be overcome to make the metaverse achievable. Today's quasi-metaverse experiences such as Roblox and Horizon Worlds are often compromised by glitches and lags. Decentraland and The Sandbox load so slowly that it's painful to browse the virtual land (the speed of course varies depending on the users' hardware and internet connection). It's frustrating to wait for the avatar to move around and for the virtual world to slowly load.

XR hardware still suffers from high prices, short battery life, discomfort, dizziness, and nausea after long usage. VR content like VR games is expensive for most people, with most games costing more than a Netflix monthly membership to access. Other technologies to enhance VR experiences like brain-machine interface, touch simulation, and the simulation of other senses are still are a long way off. These problems need to be solved and new technologies need to be invented to support more complex and realistic metaverse designs and interactions.

There is also a limit on the number of players in one virtual environment, often at dozens of players at one time, or at most, around 100 players. This limit needs to go higher to allow for more users interacting with each other in one virtual setting. In order for the metaverse to become mainstream, there should be a degree of flexibility in terms of hardware requirements so users can enjoy experiences best suited for their needs and wallets.

The technological infrastructure will need a big overhaul to deliver the metaverse. The computing capabilities for the metaverse will be "several orders of magnitude more powerful" than the current system, according to an Intel executive.[178] The "entire plumbing of the internet", from computing, storage and networking infrastructure, will need major upgrades to achieve super high bandwidths and extremely low latencies to deliver a convincing experience. All these will take time, perhaps decades, to improve.

The legal, regulatory, security, and ethical risks of the metaverse will be equally daunting. As there is currently no consensus definition of the metaverse, it's perhaps premature to discuss metaverse regulations. Regulators, however, are already paying close attention to the development and assessing the best approach. Margrethe Vestager, the executive vice president of the European Commission for A Europe Fit for the Digital Age, has expressed concerns about the regulatory implications of the metaverse: "The metaverse will present new markets and a range of different businesses. There will be a marketplace where someone may have a dominant position," referring to potential antitrust implications.[179] Chinese state media has also warned of financial and ethical risks of the metaverse.

Existing laws and regulations should apply to metaverse-related sectors such as chips, hardware, computing, algorithms, applications, wearables, and the relevant intellectual properties, patents, and products. Existing legal principles including consumer protection, IP rights, and anti-competition should apply to the metaverse. For example, advertising in the metaverse needs to follow the same rules in the physical world to be truthful and evidence-based. The U.S. Federal Trade Commission's transparency principles on native advertising (referring to ads appearing as editorial content) should extend to the metaverse. When a virtual friend tells you how wonderful their newly purchased pet cat is in Second Life, for example, you should be able to tell if they are a genuine friend or a sponsored bot trying to sell you something.

There are other legal principles that can be applied to the metaverse, like determining who has jurisdiction over virtual crimes such as theft and fraud. Avatars in quasi-metaverse experiences today already have committed fraud, theft, murder, sexual abuse, and other more egregious "virtual crimes". Because these actions take place over the internet with legal entities operating the platforms and the individuals' residences often scattered around the world, it's difficult to determine who has jurisdiction over such cases. There are ample legal principles for cyberspace jurisdiction during the Internet era that can be used for the metaverse to ensure harmful conduct can be addressed by the correct legal institutions.

Such an existing legal framework varies greatly across countries, further supporting the idea that the future metaverse ecosystem will be many virtual worlds exiting in parallel. It will be like Apple's app store having distinct versions of the app store according to the user's resident country. Creating different versions of the metaverse will be a necessity for platforms to meet local laws and regulations.

For example, cryptocurrencies and freely tradable NFTs are not permitted in China. Strict content control in China also presents challenges for Roblox-type metaverse platforms relying on user-generated content. Companies will likely incur higher costs and hurdles in content moderation in China. Chinese game companies face a tough content approval process. Regulators often require multiple amendments of games content, and are averse to extreme violence. Some games even change the blood to the color green, or skip the process of displaying players' deaths, in order to obtain approval more easily. Overall, a game in China requires a much longer time to get approved. All these increase costs and add uncertainties for game companies and create a disparate global operating environment.

As much as existing legal and regulatory principles can be applied to the metaverse, the future virtual worlds will create more scenarios testing the boundaries of current legal systems. For example, does the creation of virtual humans carry similar types of legal protections as that of a real person? If so, who should have those rights and responsibilities? How can we determine what constitutes a patent or copyright infringement in the metaverse? Who owns metaverse rights under existing contracts that were drafted before the metaverse idea was contemplated? What biometrics data can big tech companies track, and how can they use it? How do data sovereignty laws impact the sale of virtual goods across real borders?

As the metaverse will create its own economic ecosystem with virtual goods transactions amounting to large sums, it presents new challenges for regulators to police perhaps new forms of tax evasion, money laundering, virtual gambling, terrorism financing, and pyramid schemes. How governments fight financial crimes or ensure user protection on metaverse platforms where users are seemingly anonymous and transactions often cross borders will require new regulatory approaches. In all, it's predictable that as the metaverse thrives, so will legal complexities surrounding this new virtual land.

The metaverse will accentuate the problem of personal data privacy. Data tracking will significantly expand from the plain vanilla internet browsing history and personal information to more invasive tracking involving more biometrics data. Companies will track eye movement, pupil changes, head movement, hand movement, heart rate, pulse, blood pressure, facial expressions, and more. These data will help companies gauge user experiences and interests more accurately, giving companies strong incentives to collect and monetize these valuable data points.

The General Data Protection Regulation (GDPR) implemented in 2018 offers protection of individuals' control and rights over their personal data in the European Union. China implemented a Personal Information Protection Law (called China's GDPR) in 2021 to strengthen the protection of personal information. There is no federal data privacy law like the GDPR in the U.S. and current regulatory frameworks include some national laws relating to the use of data in certain industries. No matter what the current regulatory approach is in different regions, the metaverse will present new challenges in personal data privacy. The range of biometrics data that will be tracked in the metaverse is going to be highly intimate and invasive. If and where there should be boundaries of this type of tracking, how these data points can be used, and who owns this data will be challenging questions to answer.

Similarly, how to keep the data generated in the metaverse – which will be of an unprecedented scale and breadth – secure presents another challenge. Much of the personally identifiable data will be highly sensitive, such as health data (heart rate, pulse, blood pressure, and potentially mental health data) and geographical data (such as sensitive physical structures, roads, and space information). This data, if exfiltrated or inadvertently leaked, could carry more catastrophic consequences.

The ethical challenges of the metaverse create touchy issues. Proponents say that the metaverse will help solve many problems, affording people more empathy, eliminate physical distances, pulling people closer together, and even save the environment by moving many human needs (like travel and business meetings) to virtual worlds. Opponents, on the other hand, find reasons for alarm everywhere. For every positive effect of the metaverse, there are opposite unintended consequences. The metaverse could make people more empathic, but also entrench their biases. When people are pulled together closer, they could find others even more intolerable. Even if the metaverse can allow people to explore the world without physical travel, to power the metaverse would require enormous energy and create a huge amount of carbon emissions.

Video streaming and gaming are projected to make up 87% of consumer internet traffic in 2022, according to the International Energy Agency. The metaverse, therefore, can be reasonably expected to take up a similar or even bigger proportion of future internet traffic. Some estimate that an avatar consumes as much electricity as a real person living in a developing country,[180] the metaverse will need to be greener for those who can afford it to enjoy it with peace of mind.

In the metaverse, content moderation will become more problematic. There are 15,000 content moderators working at Meta (most are contracted through third-party firms). [181] Around 20,000 content moderators work at ByteDance. [182] These moderators help ensure the removal of illegal and inappropriate content, decrease disinformation, meet local laws, and adhere to regulations. The challenge of content moderation increases when the content becomes more complex. It's relatively easy to moderate text, but more difficult to moderate audio and video happening in real-time. In the metaverse, the tasks become massively complicated.

Meta has created "personal boundaries", akin to an invisible air bubble around an avatar that others can't get into, to address virtual groping in its Horizon Worlds.[183] It seems to be an easy fix, but there are still so many other types of bad behavior that it won't address. Users can still abuse others in many ways such as verbal and text abuses; hacking others' accounts; stealing virtual goods; bullying; discriminating; and shaming.

Addiction, particularly game addiction, could be a grave problem. Video gamers spent about eight hours and 27 minutes each week playing games in 2021, an increase of 14% over 2020. Binge gaming, or playing games five hours in a row, is up 13% in 2021 year-on-year.[184] More shockingly, the daily active users of Roblox, where the majority of the users are minors, spend an average of 2.6 hours per day on the platform.[185] These numbers should sound alarms to everyone. As metaverse games become even more addictive for players, this addiction problem could worsen.

Beyond gaming, a higher degree of immersion in the virtual world could harm people's physical and mental health in real life. A study found that roughly 4% of European adolescents demonstrate a pathological use of the internet that affects their life and health, while 13% of the adolescents engage in maladaptive behavior when using the internet. Similar numbers are reported for adults.[186] There have been numerous studies showing the association of anxiety, depression, and even physical ailments with the use of social media platforms.[187] All these negative effects of the internet will definitely be exacerbated in the metaverse. There is no sign that our society and the people are well prepared for these harmful consequences.

As the metaverse creates a virtual world where experiences are incrementally inching toward real-life experiences, new forms of confusing problems could arise. Is it okay for someone to create a virtual human that looks like a real-life person, and then do harmful things (beat, slap, even rape) to them in the metaverse? Or is it okay to do things that are not harmful but without the permission or acknowledgment of that person? What if an AI algorithm creates a virtual human that looks like a real person? Would any activity conducted by this virtual human be a form of infringement?

Perhaps the hardest question that the metaverse will pose to humanity is the fundamental philosophical question of what is real and what is not. Suppose technological advancements maintain upward momentum, then there will be a singularity where human senses won't be able to distinguish reality from virtual reality. Oxford faculty Nick Bostrom wrote a paper in 2003 that argues that there is a significant chance that humans are currently living in a simulation. [188] That would be the ultimate test on the foundations of human existence. Perhaps, no one is prepared for that day, yet nothing can stop people from moving toward that ultimate confusion.

References

[1] *A meta market opportunity: The metaverse could soon be worth $1 trillion.* trtworld.com. November 26, 2021 https://www.trtworld.com/magazine/a-meta-market-opportunity-the-metaverse-could-soon-be-worth-1-trillion-52067 Retrieved on March 1, 2022

[2] Mark Zuckerberg. *Remarks on the Meta (Facebook) Connect 2021 Event.* October 28, 2021 https://www.rev.com/blog/transcripts/meta-facebook-connect-2021-metaverse-event-transcript Retrieved on February 3, 2022

[3] Welsh, Oli. *Microsoft CEO argues that buying Activision Blizzard will help him build the metaverse.* Polygon.com. February 4, 2022 https://www.polygon.com/22917625/microsoft-activision-blizzard-metaverse-satya-nadella Retrieved on February 4, 2022

[4] Huddleston Jr, Tom. *Microsoft's metaverse plans are getting clearer with its $68.7 billion Activision acquisition.* cnbc.com. January 19, 2022 https://www.cnbc.com/2022/01/19/microsoft-activision-what-satya-nadella-has-said-about-the-metaverse.html Retrieved on February 4, 2022

[5] Vondale, Lisa. *Iger Offers Reflection on Metaverse, Movies and More.* Mickeyblog.com. January 28, 2022. https://mickeyblog.com/2022/01/28/iger-offers-reflection-metaverse-movies-more Retrieved on February 4, 2022

[6] Stankiewicz, Kevin. *Nvidia CEO says the metaverse could save companies billions of dollars in the real world.* cnbc.com. November 19, 2021 https://www.cnbc.com/2021/11/19/nvidia-ceo-says-the-metaverse-could-save-companies-billions.html Retrieved on February 4, 2022

[7] Hamilton, Ian. *Epic Games CEO Tim Sweeney On AR: 'We're Going To Need Very Strong Privacy Protections'.* uploadvr.com. March 26, 2019 https://uploadvr.com/tim-sweeney-ar/ Retrieved on February 7, 2022

[8] Hayward, Andrew. *'No Company Can Own' the Metaverse, Says Epic Games CEO.* decypt.co. November 17, 2021 https://decrypt.co/86323/no-company-can-own-metaverse-epic-games-ceo-tim-sweeney Retrieved on February 7, 2022

[9] Ball, Matthew. *The Metaverse: What It is, Where to Find it, and Who Will Build It.* matthewball.vc. January 13, 2020 https://www.matthewball.vc/all/themetaverse Retrieved on February 4, 2022

[10] Wen, Ting. 马化腾预判移动互联网升级方向：全真互联网(*Ma Huateng predicts the direction of mobile internet upgrade: quanzhen internet*). Xinhuanet.com. December 4, 2020 http://sh.xinhuanet.com/2020-12/04/c_139562226.htm Retrieved on February 4, 2022

[11] Guan, Xiaopu; Li, Yunshu. 元宇宙如何改写人类社会生活 (*How the Metaverse Rewrites Human Social Life*). ccdi.gov.cn. December 23, 2021 https://www.ccdi.gov.cn/toutiaon/202112/t20211223_160087.html Retrieved on February 4, 2022

[12] Metaverse is capitalized in the novel Snow Crash as it refers to a specific virtual world in the book. But the term is often not capitalized when not referring to any specific metaverse and is used to describe the concept.

[13] Stephenson, Neal. *Snow Crash.* New York: Bantam Books, 1993

[14] Terdiman, Daniel. *Counting the real 'Second Life' population.* cnet.com. January 4, 2007 https://www.cnet.com/tech/gaming/counting-the-real-second-life-population/ Retrieved on February 11, 2022

[15] *History of Virtual Reality.* vrs.org.uk. https://www.vrs.org.uk/virtual-reality/history.html Retrieved on February 8, 2022

[16] Javornik, Ana. *The Mainstreaming of Augmented Reality: A Brief History.* Harvard Business Review. October 4, 2016 https://hbr.org/2016/10/the-mainstreaming-of-augmented-reality-a-brief-history Retrieved on February 8, 2022

[17] Gill, Ryan. *1 Minute in the Metaverse Episode 1 "The Open Metaverse Promise" w/ Ryan Gill.* Linkedin.com. November 11, 2021

https://www.linkedin.com/pulse/1-minute-metaverse-episode-open-promise-w-ryan-gill-gustshow/ Retrieved on February 11, 2022

[18] *Most Played Games In 2021, Ranked by Peak Concurrent Players.* twinfinite.net. December 18, 2021 https://twinfinite.net/2021/12/most-played-games-in-2020-ranked-by-peak-concurrent-players/ Retrieved on February 9, 2022

[19] *Chainalysis: NFT market topped US$40b in 2021 | Malay Mail.* headtopics.com. January 13, 2022 https://headtopics.com/my/chainalysis-nft-market-topped-us-40b-in-2021-malay-mail-23406984 Retrieved on February 9, 2022

[20] Clement. J. *Annual growth of consume spending on in-game purchases worldwide from 2021 to 2025.* statista.com. September 7, 2021 https://www.statista.com/statistics/1240256/in-game-consumer-spending-worldwide-growth/ Retrieved on February 9, 2022

[21] *Metaverse may be $800 billion market, next tech platform.* Bloomberg. December 01, 2021 https://www.bloomberg.com/professional/blog/metaverse-may-be-800-billion-market-next-tech-platform/ Retrieved on February 9, 2022

[22] Williams, Sean. The Single Biggest Question That'll Determine the Future of the $30 Trillion Metaverse. The Motley Fool. December 14, 2021 https://www.fool.com/investing/2021/12/14/question-determine-future-of-30-trillion-metaverse/ Retrieved on February 9, 2022

[23] Roser, Max. *Extreme poverty: how far have we come, how far do we still have to go?* ourworldindata.org. November 22, 2021 https://ourworldindata.org/extreme-poverty-in-brief Retrieved on March 14, 2022

[24] Mark Zuckerberg. *Remarks on the Meta (Facebook) Connect 2021 Event.* October 28, 2021 https://www.rev.com/blog/transcripts/meta-facebook-connect-2021-metaverse-event-transcript Retrieved on February 3, 2022

[25] Mark Zuckerberg. *Remarks on the Meta (Facebook) Connect 2021 Event.* October 28, 2021 https://www.rev.com/blog/transcripts/meta-facebook-connect-2021-metaverse-event-transcript Retrieved on February 14, 2022

[26] Cava, Marco della. *Oculus cost $3B not $2B, Zuckerberg says in trial.* USA Today. January 17, 2017 https://www.usatoday.com/story/tech/news/2017/01/17/oculus-cost-3-

billion-mark-zuckerberg-trial-dallas/96676848/ Retrieved on February 14, 2022

[27] Garber, Megan. *Questions About Facebook's New Foray Into Virtual Reality*. The Atlantic. March 26, 2014 https://www.theatlantic.com/technology/archive/2014/03/whats-oculus-rift-and-other-questions-about-facebooks-new-foray-into-virtual-reality/359612/ Retrieved on February 14, 2022

[28] Popper, Ben. *Mark Zuckerberg says virtual reality is the obvious next step for Facebook*. The Verge. January 29, 2015 https://www.theverge.com/2015/7/29/9069675/mark-zuckerberg-says-virtual-reality-is-the-obvious-next-step-for Retrieved on February 14, 2022

[29] Kovach, Steve. *Mark Zuckerberg's 'metaverse' business lost more than $10 billion last year, and the losses keep growing*. CNBC.com. February 2, 2022 https://www.cnbc.com/2022/02/02/meta-reality-labs-reports-10-billion-loss.html Retrieved on February 14, 2022

[30] Byford, Sam. *Almost a fifth of Facebook employees are now working on VR and AR: report*. The Verge. March 12, 2021 https://www.theverge.com/2021/3/12/22326875/facebook-reality-labs-ar-vr-headcount-report Retrieved on February 14, 2022

[31] Sharma, Rakesh. *Will Activision Really Boost Microsoft's (MSFT) Metaverse Ambitions?* Investopedia. January 24, 2022 https://www.investopedia.com/microsoft-activision-metaverse-ambitions-5216839 Retrieved on February 15, 2022

[32] Gallagher, Dan. *Metaverse Needs More Than VR Christmas Bump*. The Wall Street Journal. January 2, 2022 https://www.wsj.com/articles/metaverse-needs-more-than-vr-christmas-bump-11641135782 Retrieved on February 14, 2022

[33] *HTC may release a VR/AR smartphone, but will there be space for it in the market? HTC 或发布 VR/AR 智能手机，市场还有它的位置吗？* sinaVR. March 7, 2022 https://vr.sina.com.cn/news/hot/2022-03-07/doc-imcwiwss4604822.shtml Retrieved on March 15, 2022

[34] Nover, Scott. *Meta's Oculus was the US's most-downloaded app on Christmas*. qz.com. December 28, 2021 https://qz.com/2107700/metas-oculus-was-the-top-app-in-the-us-on-christmas/ Retrieved on March 15, 2022

134

[35] Regalado, Antonio. *Facebook is ditching plans to make an interface that reads the brain.* The MIT Technology Review. July 14, 2021 https://www.technologyreview.com/2021/07/14/1028447/facebook-brain-reading-interface-stops-funding/ Retrieved on February 14, 2022

[36] Hayden, Scott. *Meta's 'Horizon' Social VR Platform Surpasses 300,000 Users in 3 Months.* roadtovr.com. February 18, 2022 https://www.roadtovr.com/meta-horizon-worlds-300000-users-3-months/ Retrieved on February 25, 2022

[37] Oculus app Store Preview. https://apps.apple.com/us/app/oculus/id1366478176 Retrieved on February 22, 2022

[38] *Connect 2021: Our vision for the metaverse.* October 28, 2021 https://tech.fb.com/connect-2021-our-vision-for-the-metaverse/ Retrieved on February 15, 2022

[39] Baker, Harry. *Everything You Need To Know: Facebook Login, User Data And Privacy On Meta Quest Headsets.* uploadvr.com. December 7, 2021 https://uploadvr.com/facebook-login-privacy-data-quest-2/ Retrieved on March 15, 2022

[40] *Connect 2021: Our vision for the metaverse.* October 28, 2021 https://tech.fb.com/connect-2021-our-vision-for-the-metaverse/ Retrieved on February 15, 2022

[41] Strange, Adario. We May Finally Know How Many HoloLens Devices Microsoft Sold, & It's a Revealing Peek at the Future of AR. Next Reality. April 30, 2018 https://hololens.reality.news/news/we-may-finally-know-many-hololens-devices-microsoft-sold-its-revealing-peek-future-ar-0184481/ Retrieved on February 15, 2022

[42] Novet, Jordan. *Microsoft wins U.S. Army contract for augmented reality headsets, worth up to $21.9 billion over 10 years.* CNBC.com. March 31, 2021 https://www.cnbc.com/2021/03/31/microsoft-wins-contract-to-make-modified-hololens-for-us-army.html Retrieved on February 15, 2022

[43] Bach, Deborah. *U.S. Army to use HoloLens technology in high-tech headsets for soldiers.* Microsoft.com. June 8, 2021 https://news.microsoft.com/transform/u-s-army-to-use-hololens-technology-in-high-tech-headsets-for-soldiers/ Retrived on February 15, 2022

[44] Hayden, Scott. *Report: Microsoft Braces for Negative Field Tests of Military HoloLens.* roadtovr.com. March 15, 2022 https://www.roadtovr.com/report-microsoft-hololens-ivas-field-test/ Retrieved on March 16, 2022

[45] Lang, Ben. *Meta Plans to Fuse Its 'Horizon' Apps & Make Them More Accessible... Eventually.* roadtovr.com. January 5, 2022 https://www.roadtovr.com/meta-fuse-horizon-metaverse-apps-non-vr-support/ Retrived on March 15, 2022

[46] *Decentralized Identity: Own and control your identity.* Microsoft Whitepaper. https://query.prod.cms.rt.microsoft.com/cms/api/am/binary/RE2DjfY Retrieved on February 16, 2022

[47] Fingas, J. *Apple said to have ruled out a metaverse for its mixed reality headset.* Engadget.com. January 9th, 2022 https://www.engadget.com/apple-no-metaverse-for-vr-headset-182544991.html Retrieved on February 16, 2022

[48] Tatevosian, Parkev. *Apple CEO Sees Big Potential in the Metaverse.* The Motley Fool. February 2, 2022 https://www.fool.com/investing/2022/02/02/apple-ceo-tim-cook-metaverse-interested/ Retrieved on February 16, 2022

[49] Pritchard, Tom. *Apple VR/AR headset — everything we know so far.* tom's guide. February 10, 2022 https://www.tomsguide.com/news/apple-vr-and-mixed-reality-headset-release-date-price-specs-and-leaks Retrieved on February 16, 2022

[50] Kozuch, Kate. *Apple Glasses: Everything we've heard so far.* tom's guide. February 10, 2022 https://www.tomsguide.com/news/apple-glasses Retrieved on February 16, 2022; Hector, Hamish. Apple Glass AR could create holograms of virtual objects. techadar.com March 23, 2021 https://www.techradar.com/news/apple-glass-ar-could-create-holograms-of-virtual-objects Retrieved on February 16, 2022

[51] Park, Sora; Park, Jeongeun. *Samsung vs Apple competing over metaverse devices.* Korea IT News. February 24, 2022 https://english.etnews.com/20220224200001 Retrieved on March 3, 2022

[52] Radoff, Jon. *Clash of the Metaverse Titans: Microsoft, Meta and Apple.* medium.com. November 12, 2021 https://medium.com/building-the-metaverse/clash-of-the-metaverse-titans-microsoft-meta-and-apple-ce505b010376 Retrieved on February 16, 2022

[53] reddit discussion board https://www.reddit.com/r/VRGaming/comments/j1lm7y/why_is_the_oculus_quest_2_so_cheap_compared_to/ Retrieved on February 16, 2022

[54] Li, Abner. *Sundar Pichai thinks of the metaverse as more immersive computing with AR.* 9to5google.com. November 17, 2021 https://9to5google.com/2021/11/17/sundar-pichai-google-metaverse/ Retrieved on February 17, 2022

[55] Wilde, Damien. *Google Store stops selling Cardboard VR headsets.* 9to5google.com. March 3, 2021 https://9to5google.com/2021/03/03/google-store-stops-selling-cardboard-vr-headsets/ Retrieved on February 17, 2022

[56] Kastrenakes, Jacob. *Google previews Project Starline, a next-gen 3D video chat booth.* The Verge. May 18, 2021 https://www.theverge.com/2021/5/18/22442336/google-project-starline-3d-video-chat-platform Retrieved on February 17, 2022

[57] Li, Abner. *Sundar Pichai thinks of the metaverse as more immersive computing with AR.* 9to5google.com November 15, 2021 https://9to5google.com/2021/11/17/sundar-pichai-google-metaverse/ Retrieved on February 17, 2022

[58] GPU stands for graphics processing unit, a chip specialized in computer graphics and image processing; while DPU stands for data processing unit, a programmable specialized chip for data processing.

[59] Doucet, Lars; Pecorella, Anthony. *Game engines on Steam: The definitive breakdown.* Game Developer. September 2, 2021 https://www.gamedeveloper.com/business/game-engines-on-steam-the-definitive-breakdown Retrieved on February 18, 2022

[60] Roumeliotis, Greg; Wang, Echo. *EXCLUSIVE China's Tencent in talks with U.S. to keep gaming investments -sources.* Reuters. May 5, 2021 https://www.reuters.com/technology/exclusive-chinas-tencent-talks-with-us-keep-gaming-investments-sources-2021-05-05/ Retrieved on March 15, 2022

[61] Deagon, Brian. *Roblox Stock Continues To Climb As Market Value Tops $39 Billion.* investor.com. March 11, 2021 https://www.investors.com/news/technology/roblox-ipo-trading-begins-online-gaming-value-29-billion-rblx/ Retrieved on February 18, 2022

[62] Zhang, Jinshan. *Can everything be "metaverse"?万物皆可"元宇宙"?* People's Daily. November 18, 2021

https://www.sohu.com/a/501817647_116237?spm=smpc.topic_124.tpl-pc-feed.1.1645558642993TfVhbZm_39950 Retrieved on February 22, 2022

[63] Zhou, Jing; Liu, Mingxi. *How to view the metaverse? Expert: Be wary of bubbles while staying curious* 如何看待元宇宙？专家：保持好奇心的同时警惕泡沫和忽悠 People.com.cn November 24, 2021 http://www.people.com.cn/n1/2021/1124/c32306-32290518.html Retrieved on February 22, 2022

[64] Liu, Qian. *Local governments rush into the metaverse, who can establish a first-mover advantage?* 地方政府跑步入局元宇宙 谁能建立先发优势？21 Century Economic Report. January 12, 2022 https://m.21jingji.com/article/20220112/herald/ce5353dab94ebb24bb709891ddb03626.html Retrieved on February 22, 2022

[65] New Infrastructure is an economic development concept created in 2018 during China's Central Economic Work Conference emphasizing the need for creation of new infrastructure based on hi-tech (such as 5G and big data) infrastructure, as opposed to traditional Infrastructure-based development.

[66] *A Complete List Of Venture Investments In Metaverse Startups In China: See What VCs Are Betting On.* chinamoneynetwork.com. March 15, 2022 https://www.chinamoneynetwork.com/2022/03/15/a-complete-list-of-venture-investments-in-metaverse-startups-in-china-see-what-vcs-are-betting-on Retrieved on March 15, 2022

[67] Chittum, Morgan. *Morgan Stanley Sees $8 Trillion Metaverse Market — In China Alone.* blockworks.com. February 1, 2022 https://blockworks.co/morgan-stanley-sees-8-trillion-metaverse-market-eventually/ Retrieved on March 15, 2022

[68] *Ma Huateng: Tencent has a lot of technologies and capabilities to explore and develop the "metaverse"* 马化腾：腾讯有大量探索和开发"元宇宙"的技术和能力 Cailianshe. November 11, 2021 https://www.sohu.com/a/500491155_549351 Retrieved on February 22, 2022

[69] Wang, Zixu. *Tech giants accelerate their entry, and a new round of payment wars heats up* 流量巨头加速入场 新一轮支付大战升温 Jingji Cankao Bao. February 3, 2021 http://www.xinhuanet.com/fortune/2021-02/03/c_1127057094.htm Retrieved on February 23, 2022

[70] Lei, Jianping. *Tencent quarterly report illustration: game revenue is 44.9 billion, accounting for 32% of revenue* 腾讯季报图解：游戏营收 *449* 亿 占营收比例达 *32%* Sina.com.cn. November 10, 2021 http://finance.sina.com.cn/tech/csj/2021-11-10/doc-iktzscyy4772791.shtml Retrieved on February 23, 2022

[71] Jing, He. *Roblox officially launched, Roblox embarked on a new journey* 罗布乐思正式上线，*Roblox* 踏上新征途 qq.com July 13, 2021 https://new.qq.com/omn/20210714/20210714A01D7V00.html Retrieved on February 23,2022

[72] *Announcement on the end of the Roblox deletion test* 罗布乐思删档测试结束公告 roblox.qq.com December 8, 2021 https://roblox.qq.com/web202106/news-detail.shtml?newsid=15359110 Retrieved on February 23, 2022

[73] *Official website of the Cyberspace Administration of China.* http://www.cac.gov.cn/2019zt/szcx2/index.htm Retrieved on February 23, 2022

[74] *Three years after the launch on WeGame, Fortnite announced that the server will be closed and suspended* 上线 *WeGame* 三年后《堡垒之夜》宣布关服停测 36kr.com November 1, 2021 https://www.36kr.com/p/1466190292452484 Retrieved on February 23, 2022

[75] Roumeliotis, Greg; Wang, Echo. *EXCLUSIVE China's Tencent in talks with U.S. to keep gaming investments -sources.* Reuters. May 5, 2021 https://www.reuters.com/technology/exclusive-chinas-tencent-talks-with-us-keep-gaming-investments-sources-2021-05-05/ Retrieved on March 15, 2022

[76] Gui, Zhiwei. *Tencent's first metaverse project is exposed, thousands of people gather.* 腾讯首款元宇宙项目曝光，千人集结. coreesports.net. September 29, 2021 http://www.coreesports.net/16989.html Retrieved on February 25, 2022

[77] *Black Shark acquired by tech giant, may transition to VR.* 黑鲨嫁豪门，改行做 *VR* pingwest.com. January 20, 2022 https://www.pingwest.com/a/257317 Retrieved on February 23, 2022

[78] *Black Shark acquired by tech giant, may transition to VR.* 黑鲨嫁豪门，改行做 *VR* pingwest.com. January 20, 2022
https://www.pingwest.com/a/257317 Retrieved on February 23, 2022

[79] Qiu, Xiaofen; Su, Jianxun. *Tencent takes a key step in the metaverse: it plans to acquire the game mobile phone maker Black Shark* 腾讯迈出元宇宙关键一步：拟收购游戏手机厂商黑鲨. 36kr.com. January 10, 2022
https://36kr.com/p/1563748312534921 Retrieved on February 23, 2022

[80] *Black Shark acquired by tech giant, may transition to VR.* 黑鲨嫁豪门，改行做 *VR* pingwest.com. January 20, 2022
https://www.pingwest.com/a/257317 Retrieved on February 23, 2022

[81] Kharpal, Arjun. *TikTok owner ByteDance takes first step into virtual reality with latest acquisition.* cnbc.com. August 30, 2021
https://www.cnbc.com/2021/08/30/tiktok-owner-bytedance-acquires-pico-and-takes-first-step-into-virtual-reality.html Retrieved on February 24, 2022

[82] haiyinwangyuquan. *Byte 5 billion bought Pico, is it worth the money?* 字节 50 亿买下 *Pico*，这钱花得值吗？ *August* 30, 2021
https://posts.careerengine.us/p/612d6198defe5326dac765b3 Retrieved on February 24, 2022

[83] Gartenberg, Chaim. *Meta's Oculus Quest 2 has shipped 10 million units, according to Qualcomm.* The Verge. November 16, 2021
https://www.theverge.com/2021/11/16/22785469/meta-oculus-quest-2-10-million-units-sold-qualcomm-xr2 Retrieved on February 24, 2022

[84] *ByteDance collects three tools for its metaverse.* 字节跳动悄咪咪凑齐元宇宙"三件套"Jiemian.com. February 15, 2022
https://m.jiemian.com/article/7103241.html Retrieved on February 24, 2022

[85] *An article to understand ByteDance's metaverse layout.* 一文了解字节跳动的元宇宙布局. tuoluo.com. December 9, 2021
https://www.tuoluo.cn/article/detail-10092616.html Retrieved on February 25, 2022

[86] Shen, Songlin. *Metaverse, a card that ByteDance cannot afford to lose.* 元宇宙，字节跳动不容有失的一张牌. JIemian. February 18, 2022

https://www.jiemian.com/article/7117684.html Retrieved on February 24, 2022

[87] *ByteDance's revenue this year may reach 240 billion yuan, advertising, e-commerce and live broadcasting will become the driving force* 字节跳动今年营收或将达 2400 亿 广告、电商和直播成拉动增长的三驾马车 36kr.com. November 13, 2020 https://36kr.com/p/966671022844168 Retrieved on February 24, 2022

[88] *Analysis of the 2020 annual report of China's top 20 game companies: the growth rate of top companies is improving.* 中国 20 强游戏公司 2020 年报分析：头部公司业绩增速向好 Thepaper.cn. May 21, 2021 https://www.thepaper.cn/newsDetail_forward_12767161 Retrieved on February 24,2022

[89] Reuters staff. *ByteDance acquires gaming studio Moonton at around $4 billion valuation: sources.* Reuters.com. March 22, 2021 https://www.reuters.com/article/us-bytedance-videogames-mooton-idUSKBN2BE0ES Retrieved on February 24, 2022

[90] Perez, Sarah. *TikTok is building its own AR development platform, TikTok Effect Studio.* TechCrunch. August 23, 2021 https://techcrunch.com/2021/08/23/tiktok-is-building-its-own-ar-development-platform-tiktok-effect-studio/ Retrieved on February 25, 2022

[91] https://apps.apple.com/cn/app/%E5%B8%8C%E5%A3%A4/id1578275525 Retrieved on February 28, 2022

[92] Baidu livestreaming Create 2021, provided by Baidu.

[93] Heath, Alex. *Meta opens up access to its VR social platform Horizon Worlds.* The Verge. December 9, 2021 https://www.theverge.com/2021/12/9/22825139/meta-horizon-worlds-access-open-metaverse; and https://steamcommunity.com/app/471710/discussions/0/1769259642869384003/ Retrieved on February 28, 2022

[94] https://vr.baidu.com/ Retrieved on February 28,2022

[95] Huang, Xiang. *BlueFocus Communication Group joins hands with Baidu to develop Metaverse business.* 蓝色光标牵手百度开展元宇宙业务. stcn.com. December 27, 2021

141

https://www.stcn.com/company/gsxw/202112/t20211228_4016071.html
Retrieved on February 28,2022

[96] *Alibaba Tan Ping delivered a speech: Metaverse is the next generation of Internet.* 阿里巴巴谭平发表演讲：元宇宙是下一代的互联网. Sina.com.cn. October 26, 2021 https://vr.sina.com.cn/news/hot/2021-10-26/doc-iktzscyy1828383.shtml Retrieved on March 1, 2022

[97] *The metaverse where tech giants are entering, how does Alibaba Cloud cut in from cloud games.* 巨头都在布局的元宇宙，阿里元境如何从云游戏切入.Sohu.com. December 8, 2021 https://www.sohu.com/a/506442651_204728 Retrieved on March 1, 2022

[98] *A meta market opportunity: The metaverse could soon be worth $1 trillion.* trtworld.com. November 26, 2021 https://www.trtworld.com/magazine/a-meta-market-opportunity-the-metaverse-could-soon-be-worth-1-trillion-52067 Retrieved on March 1, 2022

[99] *The metaverse where tech giants are entering, how does Alibaba Cloud cut in from cloud games.* 巨头都在布局的元宇宙，阿里元境如何从云游戏切入 .Sohu.com. December 8, 2021 https://www.sohu.com/a/506442651_204728 Retrieved on March 1, 2022

[100] CIW Team. *China cloud computing market in Q3 2021; top 4 have 80% market share.* China Internet Watch. December 11, 2021 https://www.chinainternetwatch.com/30820/cloud-infrastructure-services/ Retrieved on March 1, 2022

[101] Li, Peijuan. *Ten pictures to understand the background and development trend of the "three-player" competition pattern of smart speakers in China in 2021.* 十张图了解2021年中国智能音箱"三足鼎立"竞争格局形成背景及发展趋势. Qianzhan Industry Research Institute. September 1, 2021 https://www.qianzhan.com/analyst/detail/220/210901-9b60851d.html Retrieved on March 1, 2022

[102] Xiao, Gongzi. *NetEase investor meeting was held in Metaverse "Yaotai", CEO Ding Lei's avatar image appeared.* 网易投资者沟通会在元宇宙"瑶台"举办，CEO 丁磊虚拟人形象现身.IThome.com. December23, 2021 https://www.ithome.com/0/594/212.htm Retrieved on March 7, 2022

[103] Yang, Guiyu. *NetEase will set up Hainan headquarters in Sanya to jointly build an industrial base project with the government.* 网易将在三亚设立海南总部 与政府共建产业基地项目. Xinhuanet. December 26, 2021

http://m.news.cn/hq/2021-12/26/c_1128201942.htm Retrieved on March 1, 2022

[104] Gui, Zhiwei. *Huawe metaverse three priorities: hardware, engine, and games. 华为 Metaverse 三板斧：硬件、引擎、游戏.* coreesports.net. May 14, 2021 http://www.coreesports.net/15646.html Retrieved on March 16, 2022

[105] Patel, Vinay. *2nd Generation Huawei VR Glass To Launch Before 2021 Ends.* gizchina.com. October 24, 2021 https://www.gizchina.com/2021/10/24/2nd-generation-huawei-vr-glass-to-launch-before-2021-ends/ Retrieved on March 15, 2022

[106] Gui, Zhiwei. *Huawe metaverse three priorities: hardware, engine, and games. 华为 Metaverse 三板斧：硬件、引擎、游戏.* coreesports.net. May 14, 2021 http://www.coreesports.net/15646.html Retrieved on March 16, 2022

[107] How did consumer VR brands performed in 2021? *2021 消费市场「收官战」落幕：各大 VR 品牌的表现怎么样？*163.com. January 5, 2022 https://www.163.com/dy/article/GSUIUKK805269O3G.html Retrieved on March 16, 2022

[108] Feltham, Jamie. *More Than 50% Of VR Headsets Used On Steam Are Quests.* uploadvr.com. March 8, 2022 https://uploadvr.com/steam-quest-usage-half/ Retrieved on March 16, 2022

[109] Viverse official site. https://www.vive.com/us/viverse/ Retrieved on March 16, 2022

[110] GlobalData; Thematic Research. *South Korea: A metaverse superpower in the making?* Verdict. January 28, 2022 https://www.verdict.co.uk/south-korea-metaverse/ Retrieved on March 2, 2022

[111] GlobalData; Thematic Research. *South Korea: A metaverse superpower in the making?* Verdict. January 28, 2022 https://www.verdict.co.uk/south-korea-metaverse/ Retrieved on March 2, 2022

[112] Gaubert, Julie. *Seoul to become the first city to enter the metaverse. What will it look like?* euronews.next. November 11, 2021 https://www.euronews.com/next/2021/11/10/seoul-to-become-the-first-city-to-enter-the-metaverse-what-will-it-look-like Retrieved on March 2, 2022

143

[113] *Leading gaming markets worldwide in 2020, by gaming revenue.* Statista.com. https://www.statista.com/statistics/308454/gaming-revenue-countries/ Retrieved on March 2, 2022

[114] Shead, Sam. *Samsung held an event in the metaverse. And it didn't quite go to plan.* cnbc.com. February 10, 2022 https://www.cnbc.com/2022/02/10/samsung-held-an-event-in-the-metaverse-and-it-didnt-quite-go-to-plan.html Retrieved on March 2, 2022

[115] Eadicicco, Lisa. *The race to build AR glasses is heating up, and Samsung is surprisingly quiet.* cnet.com. January 17, 2022 https://www.cnet.com/tech/mobile/the-race-to-build-ar-glasses-is-heating-up-and-samsung-is-surprisingly-quiet/ Retrieved on March 2, 2022; Hayden, Scott. *Samsung's Leaked AR Concept Videos Reveal Its Augmented Ambitions.* roadtovr.com. February 22, 2021 https://www.roadtovr.com/leak-samsung-ar-glasses-smart-concept/ Retrieved on March 2, 2022

[116] Park, Sora; Park, Jeongeun. *Samsung vs Apple competing over metaverse devices.* Korea IT News. February 24, 2022 https://english.etnews.com/20220224200001 Retrieved on March 3, 2022

[117] Nishino, Hideaki. *First look: the headset design for PlayStation VR2.* playstation.com. February 22, 2022 https://blog.playstation.com/2022/02/22/first-look-the-headset-design-for-playstation-vr2/ Retrieved on March 2, 2022

[118] Hayward, Andrew. *Nintendo Sees 'Great Potential' in the Metaverse—But It's in No Rush, Says President.* decrypt.co February 4, 2022 https://decrypt.co/92124/nintendo-great-potential-metaverse Retrieved on March 2, 2022

[119] Saenz, Aaron. *160,000+ Watch Virtual Popstar Hatsune Miku Return to the Stage.* singularityhub.com. April 12, 2011. https://singularityhub.com/2011/04/12/160000-watch-virtual-popstar-hatsune-miku-return-to-the-stage-video-2/ Retrieved on March 2, 2022

[120] *India Set To Drive the $800 Billion Metaverse Boom.* Indianretailer.com. January 17, 2022 https://www.indianretailer.com/news/india-set-to-drive-the-800-billion-metaverse-boom.n12523/ Retrieved on March 21, 2022

[121] Stolton, Samuel. *Vestager: Metaverse poses new competition challenges.* Politico. January 18, 2022 https://www.politico.eu/article/metaverse-new-competition-challenges-margrethe-vestager/ Retrieved on March 2, 2022

[122] Clegg, Nick. *Investing in European Talent to Help Build the Metaverse.* Meta. October 17, 2021 https://about.fb.com/news/2021/10/creating-jobs-europe-metaverse/ Retrieved on March 2, 2022

[123] *Reality check.* accenture.com. https://www.accenture.com/in-en/insights/technology/interactive-xr-report Retrieved on March 3, 2022

[124] Market Research Future. *Extended Reality (XR) Market Size to Reach USD 393 Billion by 2025 at 69.4% CAGR - Report by Market Research Future (MRFR).* August 9, 2021. https://www.globenewswire.com/news-release/2021/08/09/2277296/0/en/Extended-Reality-XR-Market-Size-to-Reach-USD-393-Billion-by-2025-at-69-4-CAGR-Report-by-Market-Research-Future-MRFR.html Retrieved on March 3, 2022

[125] Hong, Yuhan. *Let's hope this is the "last" VR year. 但愿这是最后一个"VR 元年".* pingwest.com. February 7, 2022 https://www.pingwest.com/a/253750 Retrieved on March 3, 2022

[126] *Extended Reality (XR) Market Research Report.* https://www.psmarketresearch.com/market-analysis/extended-reality-xr-market-insights Retrieved on March 3, 3022

[127] This proprietary data is provided by Omdia directly.

[128] Gallagher, Dan. *Metaverse Needs More Than VR Christmas Bump.* The Wall Street Journal. January 2, 2022 https://www.wsj.com/articles/metaverse-needs-more-than-vr-christmas-bump-11641135782 Retrieved on February 14, 2022

[129] Regalado, Antonio. *Facebook is ditching plans to make an interface that reads the brain.* The MIT Technology Review. July 14, 2021 https://www.technologyreview.com/2021/07/14/1028447/facebook-brain-reading-interface-stops-funding/ Retrieved on February 14, 2022

[130] VIAR. The state of the VR headset market at the end of 2021. viar360.com. https://www.viar360.com/the-state-of-the-vr-headset-market-at-the-end-of-2021/ Retrieved on March 3, 2022

[131] Lina. *Pico launches Neo 3 VR device with Qualcomm XR2 chip at RMB2,499. Pico 推出 Neo 3 系列VR 一体机，搭载高通XR2 芯片，售价 2499 元起.*36kr.com. May 10, 2021 https://www.36kr.com/p/1218625591562887 Retrieved on March 3, 2022

[132] VIAR. The state of the VR headset market at the end of 2021. viar360.com. https://www.viar360.com/the-state-of-the-vr-headset-market-at-the-end-of-2021/ Retrieved on March 3, 2022 Note: these ranking changes quickly, and HTC and Sony rounded out as the top 5 VR headset companies after Oculus, DPVR, Pico.

[133] Gui, Zhiwei. *Huawe metaverse three priorities: hardware, engine, and games. 华为Metaverse 三板斧：硬件、引擎、游戏.* coreesports.net. May 14, 2021 http://www.coreesports.net/15646.html Retrieved on March 16, 2022

[134] Patel, Vinay. *2nd Generation Huawei VR Glass To Launch Before 2021 Ends.* gizchina.com. October 24, 2021 https://www.gizchina.com/2021/10/24/2nd-generation-huawei-vr-glass-to-launch-before-2021-ends/ Retrieved on March 15, 2022

[135] How did consumer VR brands performed in 2021? *2021 消费市场「收官战」落幕：各大 VR 品牌的表现怎么样？*163.com. January 5, 2022 https://www.163.com/dy/article/GSUIUKK805269O3G.html Retrieved on March 16, 2022

[136] Feltham, Jamie. *More Than 50% Of VR Headsets Used On Steam Are Quests.* uploadvr.com. March 8, 2022 https://uploadvr.com/steam-quest-usage-half/ Retrieved on March 16, 2022

[137] *Huawei HiSilicon releases XR mixed reality chip: supports 8K decoding, integrates GPU, NPU. 华为海思发布XR 混合现实芯片：支持8K 解码，集成 GPU、NPU.* 21ic.com. June 11, 2020 https://www.21ic.com/article/780228.html Retrieved on March 4, 2022

[138] Hong, Yuhan. *Let's hope this is the "last" VR year. 但愿这是最后一个"VR 元年".* pingwest.com. February 7, 2022 https://www.pingwest.com/a/253750 Retrieved on March 3, 2022

[139] Peng, Baoxuan. *Spin-off subsidiary of GoerTek goes public. 分拆子公司歌尔微上市 歌尔股份踏入 VR 赛道营收大增背后.* Sohu.com. November 18, 2021 https://www.sohu.com/a/501802917_161105 Retrieved on March 4, 2022

[140] *Global Game Engines Market 2022: Growth Analysis, Opportunities, Developments and Forecast to 2024 | Impressive Growth Rate and Business Prospect, Historical Analysis, New Product Launches.* marketwatch.com. March 4, 2022 https://www.marketwatch.com/press-release/global-game-

engines-market-2022-growth-analysis-opportunities-developments-and-forecast-to-2024-impressive-growth-rate-and-business-prospect-historical-analysis-new-product-launches-2022-03-04 Retrieved on March 4, 2022

[141] Dillet, Romain. *Unity CEO says half of all games are built on Unity.* TechCrunch. September 5, 2018 https://techcrunch.com/2018/09/05/unity-ceo-says-half-of-all-games-are-built-on-unity/ Retrieved on March 4, 2022

[142] Takahashi, Dean. *Unity's first post-IPO report: Revenue jumps 53% to $200.8 million.* venturebeat.com. November 12, 2020 https://venturebeat.com/2020/11/12/unitys-first-post-ipo-report-revenue-jumps-53-to-200-8-million/ Retrieved on March 4, 2022

[143] *Max Hu's Annual China Macro Update + Unity Software Thesis.* moiglobal.com. April 14, 2021 https://moiglobal.com/max-hu-202104/ Retrieved on March 4, 2022

[144] Liangzi; Long, Zhixin. *Unity Zhang Junbo interview: global team of 4,000; aiming for more AAA games.* 专访 Unity 张俊波：全球团队近 4000 人，瞄准更多 3A 游戏.xueqiu.com. August 2, 2020 https://xueqiu.com/1058212218/155571724 Retrieved on March 4, 2022

[145] Takahashi, Dean. *Cocos adds 3D to its open source 2D game engine with Cocos Creator 3.0.* venturebeat.com. February 8, 2021 https://venturebeat.com/2021/02/08/cocos-adds-3d-to-its-open-source-2d-game-engine-with-cocos-creator-3-0/ Retrieved on March 4, 2022

[146] *China's mobile game revenue list released in September 2021, domestic game engine Cocos once again attracted attention.* 2021 年 9 月中国手游收入榜单发布，国产游戏引擎 Cocos 再度引发关注. chinadaily.com.cn. October 21, 2021 http://ex.chinadaily.com.cn/exchange/partners/82/rss/channel/cn/columns/sz8srm/stories/WS616fa667a3107be4979f3a7a.html Retrieved on March 4, 2022

[147] Takahashi, Dean. *Cocos adds 3D to its open source 2D game engine with Cocos Creator 3.0.* venturebeat.com. February 8, 2021 https://venturebeat.com/2021/02/08/cocos-adds-3d-to-its-open-source-2d-game-engine-with-cocos-creator-3-0/ Retrieved on March 4, 2022

[148] *How the "slow" game engine industry supports the games sector.* 一个慢热的引擎产业，是如何"玩"转游戏圈的？ Sohu.com. December 10, 2021 https://www.sohu.com/a/507063413_323203 Retrieved on March 7, 2022

[149] *Framing the Future of Web 3.0 Metaverse Edition.* Goldman Sachs. December10,2021 https://www.goldmansachs.com/insights/pages/gs-research/framing-the-future-of-web-3.0-metaverse-edition/report.pdf Retrieved on March 18,2022

[150] A. Hilton, D. Beresford, T. Gentils, R. Smith and Wei Sun. *Virtual people: capturing human models to populate virtual worlds.* Proceedings Computer Animation 1999, 1999, pp. 174-185, doi: 10.1109/CA.1999.781210.

[151] *Watch Epic Games level the uncanny valley in incredible MetaHuman Creator video.* inverse.com. February 10, 2021 https://www.inverse.com/gaming/unreal-engine-metahuman-creator-trailer Retrieved on March 7, 2022

[152] Xing, Xiaonan. *Microsoft Xiaoice valuation reaches over unicorn level. CEO Li Di: This Winter Olympics may not have real human referees* 微软小冰估值超独角兽，CEO 李迪：这次冬奥会，裁判可能"不是人类" sina.com. July 20,2021 https://finance.sina.com.cn/stock/usstock/c/2021-07-20/doc-ikqciyzk6539955.shtml Retrieved on March 18, 2022

[153] Zhang, Lin. *"Zhongke Shenzhi" completed the B round of financing and used AI image data-driven technology to create a content production center in the Metaverse.* 「中科深智」完成 B 轮融资，利用 AI 影像数据驱动技术打造元宇宙内容生产中台. 36kr.com. November 1, 2021 https://36kr.com/p/1466286585187335 Retrieved on March 7, 2022

[154] TF Securities. *Virtual Digital Person: The Main Character of the Metaverse.* January 20, 2022. P1

[155] Liu, Yan. *Next Generation Research: Virtual Idol Market .*次世代专题研究：虚拟偶像市场. sina.com.cn. November 2, 2021 https://stock.finance.sina.com.cn/stock/go.php/vReport_Show/kind/industry/rptid/689191546328/index.phtml Retrieved on March 7, 2022

[156] Smith, Dale; Tibken, Shara. *Samsung's Neon 'artificial humans' are confusing everyone. We set the record straight.* cnet.com. January 19, 2020. https://www.cnet.com/tech/mobile/samsung-neon-artificial-humans-are-confusing-everyone-we-set-record-straight/ Retrieved on March 7, 2022

[157] Saenz, Aaron. *160,000+ Watch Virtual Popstar Hatsune Miku Return to the Stage.* singularityhub.com. April 12, 2011. https://singularityhub.com/2011/04/12/160000-watch-virtual-popstar-hatsune-miku-return-to-the-stage-video-2/ Retrieved on March 2, 2022

[158] Decentraland price. Coinbase.com
https://www.coinbase.com/price/decentraland Retrieved on March 8, 2022

[159] *Decentraland Stats: 300K Monthly Active Users, Under 20K Daily Users.* New World Notes. December 7, 2021
https://nwn.blogs.com/nwn/2021/12/decentraland-blockchain-metaverse-user-revenue-stats.html Retrieved on March 8, 2022

[160] Sandbox price. Coinbase.com https://www.coinbase.com/price/the-sandbox Retrieved on March 8, 2022

[161] Takashi, Dean. *The Sandbox metaverse hits 2M users and launches Alpha Season 2.* venturebeat.com. March 3, 2022.
https://venturebeat.com/2022/03/03/the-sandbox-metaverse-hits-2m-users-and-launches-alpha-season-2/#:~:text=The%20Sandbox%20Alpha%20Season%202,a%20time%2Dtraveling%20tour%20of Retrieved on March 8, 2022

[162] Quiroz-Gutierrez, Marco. These little-known types of coins are being touted as crypto to watch for 2022. Fortune.com. February 17, 2022
https://fortune.com/2022/02/17/metaverse-crypto-sand-mana-to-watch-for-2022/ Retrieved on March 8, 2022

[163] Wang, Manhua. *What is Honnverse? Why a public letter is worth nearly RMB5 billion"虹宇宙"是啥？一封公开信就能价值近 50 亿.* chinaventure.com. November 23, 2021
https://www.chinaventure.com.cn/news/80-20211123-365723.html Retrieved on March 8, 2022

[164] Cailanshe. *Metaverse virtual land encounters first winter, prices drop from 180,000 to 18 yuan. 价格从 18 万跌到18 元，元宇宙虚拟房地产遭遇"第一场寒冬"*qq.com.
https://new.qq.com/omn/20220212/20220212A0A3WX00.html Retrieved on March 8, 2022

[165] Liao, Lu. *Metaverse digital community "enables" real economy in innovative marketing. Honnverse partners with Jingneng Longhuxi. 元宇宙数字社区赋能实体经济创新营销 虹宇宙与京能龙湖熙上达成合作.* chinanews.com.cn. March 1, 2022
https://www.sh.chinanews.com.cn/chanjing/2022-03-01/96454.shtml Retrieved on March 9, 2022

[166] Li, Yinchao. Total transaction value of RMB87.5 billion. e-CNY is walking into daily life with personal wallet of 261 million. 交易额达 875 亿！数字人

民币走入日常，个人钱包已开立 2.61 亿个，你感受到了吗？stcn.com. January 23, 2022 https://www.stcn.com/xw/sd/202201/t20220123_4101334.html Retrieved on March 9, 2022

[167] Brooks, Khristopher. *Bitcoin has its own 1% who control outsized share of wealth.* cbsnews.com. December 21, 2021 https://www.cbsnews.com/news/bitcoin-cryptocurrency-wealth-one-percent/ Retrieved on March 18,2022

[168] Si, Linwei. *How China's blockchain technology should development under the high pressure of cryptocurrency crackdown? 高压打击虚拟货币之下，中国的区块链技术该如何发展？* Jiemian.com. November 27, 2021 https://m.jiemian.com/article/6856275.html Retrieved on March 9, 2022

[169] JPMorgan. *Opportunities in the metaverse.* https://www.jpmorgan.com/content/dam/jpm/treasury-services/documents/opportunities-in-the-metaverse.pdf Retrieved on March 10, 2022

[170] Chittum, Morgan. *Morgan Stanley Sees $8 Trillion Metaverse Market — In China Alone.* blockworks. February 1, 2022 https://blockworks.co/morgan-stanley-sees-8-trillion-metaverse-market-eventually Retrieved on March 10, 2022

[171] *A List Of Chinese Venture Capital Investments In Metaverse Companies 2021-2022.* chinamoneynetwork.com. February 22, 2022 https://www.chinamoneynetwork.com/2022/02/22/a-list-of-chinese-venture-capital-investments-in-metaverse-companies-2021-2022 Retrieved on March 11, 2022

[172] *Huiye Tech receives several million USD in pre-A funding from Shunwei Capital. 慧夜科技完成数百万美元 Pre-A 轮融资，顺为资本独家投资.* Lieyunwang.com. January 21, 2022 https://m.lieyunwang.com/archives/480423 Retrieved on March 11, 2022

[173] *In-Game Advertising Market to reach USD 18.41 billion by 2027, is Going to Boom with RapidFire Inc., Playwire Media LLC, Atlas Alpha Inc., Engage.* October 4, 2021 http://ipsnews.net/business/2021/10/04/in-game-advertising-market-to-reach-usd-18-41-billion-by-2027-is-going-to-boom-with-rapidfire-inc-playwire-media-llc-atlas-alpha-inc-engage/ Retrieved on March 11, 2022

[174] Columbus, Louis. *BMW uses Nvidia's Omniverse to build state-of-the-art factories*. venturebeat.com. Novembe 16, 2021 https://venturebeat.com/2021/11/16/bmw-uses-nvidias-omniverse-to-build-state-of-the-art-factories/ Retrieved on March 11, 2022

[175] Kerris, Richard. *Siemens Energy Taps NVIDIA to Develop Industrial Digital Twin of Power Plant in Omniverse*. nvidia.com. November 15, 2021 https://blogs.nvidia.com/blog/2021/11/15/siemens-energy-nvidia-industrial-digital-twin-power-plant-omniverse/ Retrieved on March 11, 2022

[176] *The Use of Digital Twins for Urban Planning to Yield US$280 Billion in Cost Savings By 2030*. July 28, 2021 https://www.abiresearch.com/press/use-digital-twins-urban-planning-yield-us280-billion-cost-savings-2030/ Retrieved on March 11, 2022

[177] *How much does employee training really cost?* ELM Learning. February 24, 2022 https://elmlearning.com/blog/how-much-does-employee-training-really-cost/ Retrieved on March 11, 2022

[178] Koduri, Raja. *Powering the Metaverse*. intel.com. December 14, 2021 https://www.intel.com/content/www/us/en/newsroom/opinion/powering-metaverse.html#gs.t4mkwg Retrieved on March 14, 2022

[179] Stolton, Samuel. *Vestager: Metaverse poses new competition challenges*. Politico. January 18, 2022 https://www.politico.eu/article/metaverse-new-competition-challenges-margrethe-vestager/ Retrieved on March 2, 2022

[180] *Avatars consume as much electricity as Brazilians*. Nicholas Carr's blog. Decembe 5, 2006. https://www.roughtype.com/?p=611 Retrieved on March 21, 2022

[181] Leskin, Paige. *Facebook content moderator who quit reportedly wrote a blistering letter citing 'stress induced insomnia' among other 'trauma'*. BusinessInsider.com. April 14, 2021 https://www.businessinsider.com/facebook-content-moderator-quit-with-blistering-letter-citing-trauma-2021-4 Retrieved on March 21, 2022

[182] Ba, Jiuling. *Dozens of thousands of internet security police have been trapped inside big tech firms' precision performance metrics . 十几万"互联网保安"，被大厂的系统精算了*. Wuxiaobo Wechat Public Account. February 16, 2022 https://posts.careerengine.us/p/620cb76d5489856a243d1130 Retrieved on March 21, 2022

[183] Iovine, Anna. *Meta has a fix for virtual groping in its social VR space, Horizon Worlds.* mashable.com. February 5, 2022 https://mashable.com/article/meta-personal-boundary-horizon-worlds-facebook Retrieved on March 21, 2022

[184] Combs, Veronica. *8 hours and 27 minutes. That's how long the average gamer plays each week.* techrepublic.com. March 10, 2021 https://www.techrepublic.com/article/8-hours-and-27-minutes-thats-how-long-the-average-gamer-plays-each-week/ Retrieved on March 21, 2022

[185] Dean, Brian. *Roblox User and Growth Stats 2022.* backlinko.com. January 5, 2022 https://backlinko.com/roblox-users Retrieved on March 21, 2022

[186] Quaglio, Gianluca. *How the internet can harm us, and what can we do about it?* European Parliamentary Research Service. February 18, 2019 https://epthinktank.eu/2019/02/18/how-the-internet-can-harm-us-and-what-can-we-do-about-it/ Retrieved on March 21, 2022

[187] *The Social Dilemma: Social Media and Your Mental Health.* McLean Hospital. https://www.mcleanhospital.org/essential/it-or-not-social-medias-affecting-your-mental-health Retrieved on March 21, 2022

[188] Bostrom, NIck. *ARE YOU LIVING IN A COMPUTER SIMULATION?* Philosophical Quarterly (2003) Vol. 53, No. 211, pp. 243-255. https://www.simulation-argument.com/simulation.html Retrieved on March 21, 2022

Printed in Great Britain
by Amazon

82297685R00088